Irawati Karve (1905 [illegible]
educated in Pune. A M[illegible] ogy from
Bombay in 1928 and a [illegible] in Anthropology
from Berlin in 1930 ma[illegible] the onset of a long and distinguished career of pioneering research. She wrote in both English and Marathi, on academic subjects as well as on topics of general interest, and thus commanded an enviably wide circle of readership. Whether through her *Hindu Society: An Interpretation*, a scholarly treatise in English, or through *Yuganta: The End of an Epoch*, her study in Marathi of the characters and society in the Mahabharata, we obtain ample illustration of the range and quality of Irawati Karve's mind.

Irawati Karve (1905-1970) was born in Burma and educated in Pune. A Master's degree in Sociology from Bombay in 1928 and a Doctoral degree in Anthropology from Berlin in 1930 marked the onset of a long and distinguished career of pioneering research. She wrote in both English and Marathi on academic subjects as well as on topics of general interest and thus commanded an unusually wide circle of readership, whether through her *Hindu Society: an Interpretation*, a scholarly treatise in English, or through *Yuganta: The end of an Epoch*, her study in Marathi of the characters and society in the Mahabharata, we obtain ample illustration of the range and quality of Irawati Karve's mind.

Yuganta

The End of an Epoch

Irawati Karve

Orient BlackSwan

YUGANTA

ORIENT BLACKSWAN PRIVATE LIMITED

Registered Office
3-6-752, Himayatnagar, Hyderabad 500 029, Telangana, India
e-mail: centraloffice@orientblackswan.com

Other Offices
Bengaluru, Chennai, Guwahati, Hyderabad, Kolkata,
Mumbai, New Delhi, Noida, Patna, Visakhapatnam

Published in Sangam Books, 1974
Based on an earlier version
Published by Deshmukh Prakashan, 1969
Published by Disha Books, 1991
Reprinted 1993, 1999, 2005, 2006 (twice), 2007
First published by Orient Blackswan Private Limited 2008
Reprinted 2013, 2014, 2015, 2021

ISBN 978 81 250 1424 9

033729

Printed in India at
Yash Printographics
Greater Noida 201 310

Published by
Orient Blackswan Private Limited
3-6-752, Himayatnagar, Hyderabad 500 029, Telangana, India
e-mail: info@orientblackswan.com

Publisher's Note

This publication is in effect the second and a revised edition of the English version of *Yuganta*, the Marathi original of which was published in 1967 and subsequently won a Sahitya Akademi prize as the best book in Marathi for that year.

The first English version, published by Deshmukh Prakashan (who had published the Marathi original) in 1969, was prepared mainly for a foreign audience. As stated by the author in her preface to the volume, 'The idea of writing my Mahabharata studies in English occurred to me first when friends and pupils in the U.S.A. showed an interest in the subject. The venture has at last been completed, thanks to my American and Indian daughters, Maxine, Jai and Gauri.' The English version is not, therefore, a literal translation of the Marathi original but has been rewritten wherever necessary. Explanatory parentheses and footnotes were added to the text; six appendices provided mainly for the reader abroad; the introduction enlarged to include a summary of the epic narrative and other descriptive comments. Finally, Professor W. Norman Brown of the University of Pennsylvania wrote a foreword (a few sentences from which have been quoted on the back cover) which introduced the subject and the author to the foreign reader. The fly-leaf preceding each of the eleven chapters of text carried a line-drawing made from photographs of sculptures in temples. A note on these illustrations points out that 'the Mahabharata is rarely depicted in temples, while for the Ramayana there are hundreds of such sculptures'.

Much of this additional material has been omitted in preparing a paperback edition of the English version meant mainly for Indian readers. The author's brief preface and Professor Norman Brown's long foreword have been dropped. The Marathi original carries a *nivedan* (acknowledgements) and a *prastavana* (preface). The first five paragraphs of the latter have been translated into English and used here as the preface. The Introduction (Chapter 1 of the first English edition) has been reduced to the present form for inclusion here, by leaving out explanatory matter which presumably is not necessary for readers at home. Of the appendices, only the genealogical charts and the map have been retained.

These changes have been approved by Dr D. D. Karve, the late Irawati's husband, while their elder daughter Mrs Jai Nimbkar has prepared the translation from the Marathi preface.

The text of Chapters 2-11 remains the same as in the first edition, except for alterations in typography effected in an effort to simplify and make consistent the style of italicization and capitalization of 'Indian' words. For example, frequently occurring terms such as dharma, guru, rishi, etc., have not been italicized after their first appearance. Such liberties may offend the orthodox but it is hoped that the general reader will experience no difficulty.

Preface*

The second essay in this book was written in July 1962. I had no idea at the time that I would write any more essays about characters in the Mahabharata. However, in the next five years one essay led to another and that to the next. When each essay was finished, there was no plan for the next essay. On the other hand, I cannot say that the publication of this book means the end of these essays. With the completion of each essay I felt that it was the last, that any further writing would only be repetitive, and should not be done. At this moment I feel the same. Whether the feeling lasts or whether I shall write more cannot be predicted at this time. It is not possible to answer the question many of my friends ask me — why did I write these essays? As far as I am concerned, there is only one purpose behind speech or writing — to communicate to others something one feels strongly. This is an irrepressible primary impulse. These writings have not, as far as I am aware, been motivated by anything more. A teacher by profession, I

---

* This is a translation and adaptation of the first part of the Preface which appears in the original Marathi edition.

naturally want to be understood as fully as possible. I am therefore very particular about lucidity in writing. I do not feel sorry if, after understanding me fully, a reader finds anything wrong or objectionable in my writing and points it out to me. However, I do feel sorry if, perhaps because of careless writing, something I have written is misinterpreted.

These essays are based on the critical edition of the Mahabharata published by the Bhandarkar Oriental Research Institute. This explains why a number of things which have been popularly accepted as part of the Mahabharata have been omitted. The critical edition however, does include certain parts which are obviously later interpolations. The reason for this is that this edition is based on the manuscript which was judged the oldest among the many which were scrutinized. Parts which were entirely absent in the oldest text but present or partly present in any of the newer editions were deleted. Thus what the critical edition gives us is what the editors found in the oldest available manuscript. This however does not date further back than the eighth or ninth century A.D. The critical edition can now become the basis for further research and study.

So far the research has been based mainly on the external form of the text. This is why the critical edition has many parts which have been obviously interpolated later, and which have no connection with the story. These need to be studied and excluded. This may force the deletion of a lot that now forms part of the critical edition, and yield another revised critical edition. The process need not stop here. It may even be possible to go further and establish the text of the original book called *Jaya* which was the source of the Mahabharata. Continuing research gives us newer methods of research and helps us find the errors committed by researchers of the older generations. No specific piece of research, therefore, can be considered the last word on a subject.

Sanskrit is not my field of study. I read the Mahabharata because I like it. In these essays I have referred to several parts of the Mahabharata as interpolated. Such references are based only on my own impression formed while reading the Mahabharata. The impression is not based on research. If such parts are proved by later research to be not interpolations at all, then to that extent my interpretations must be considered wrong. Otherwise a reader can only say that he does not agree with my interpretation, not that it is necessarily wrong. The Mahabharata is an inexhaustible mine. There are various ways of making it yield its riches. No one person can encompass it entirely. Everyone uses part of this cultural wealth according to his own ability. Students of astrology, linguistics, archaeology can write about the people and events in the Mahabharata from entirely different angles. I have written according to my own ability and inclination. Some ideas I have barely touched on (e.g., what could *ajya* or *ghrita* have meant), and not researched. I have mentioned this for the benefit of some young reader who might get interested in this type of research, follow it up and make up for the deficiencies in my writing.

After the essay 'Gandhari' was published, a young Indian friend asked me, 'Who on earth was this Gandhari?' The question made me sad. I felt that I was useless in this age, merely an impediment, because I lived in the past. In a moment of weariness I even felt that I should stop writing altogether. Alternatively, I felt that I should give the whole story of the Mahabharata in the Introduction. But, after thinking them over, I abandoned both alternatives. I am a very obstinate person. The younger generation is constantly trying to convert me to their point of view. I am for ever meeting the assault of my three very modern children and my young Ph.D. students. These essays are in a way an attempt to make the younger generation understand my point of view. I shall consider it a victory if they think that my interpretation is wrong and read the Mahabharata merely to prove it wrong.

I.K.

Contents

YUGANTA - the end of an epoch

The Mahabharata thus marks the end of a Yuga. 'Yuga' in the modern languages stands generally for an era, epoch or age. I have used the word yuga in the title in this modern sense.

- Irawati Karve

1 Introduction*

'Mahabharata' is the name of a book in the Sanskrit language telling in very simple verse form the story of a family quarrel ending in a fierce battle. To this author, and to Indians in general, this is not an imaginary, made-up story, but represents a real event which took place about 1000 B.C. In the course of this narration, stories of the ancestors of the heroes who fought the battle are given. These heroes were princes who ruled at a city called Hastinapura, situated somewhere near modern Delhi. The most illustrious king among these ancestors was Bharata (the son of King Dushyanta or Dushmanta, and Shakuntala). From the name Bharata is derived the word 'bharata', which might mean: (a) 'any descendant of Bharata', or (b) 'any other aspect of Bharata', as for example a poem. *Maha* means 'the great'. The word 'Mahabharata' lets us recognize stages in the making of this poem. Perhaps there was a simpler and less extensive story called Bharata and then, by century-long accretions, it became a Maha (the great)

---

* This chapter has been adapted from the Introduction provided by the author for the English version published in 1969.

bharata (book about the descendants of Bharata).

The present version of the book, however, lets one know that there was a still earlier time when the narration had the much shorter and simpler name, *Jaya* (victory). This means that in its earliest form the narration was a poem of triumph, and told of the victory of a particular king over his rival kinsmen. Very probably it was sung by bards at the court of the king and, as the narration itself says, was also sung by wandering minstrels and eagerly listened to by the people. In the story as it is preserved, the chief narrators are different bards called *sutas*.

A class of people called sutas, representing the illegitimate progeny of the *Kshatriyas*, performed various functions at the court. They were counsellors and friends of kings, charioteers, and also bards. Some of them moved from place to place, wherever they knew that people were likely to assemble, and told their stories which consisted mainly of exploits of love and adventure of ancient and ruling kings and princes. A book in many respects like the Mahabharata was the Ramayana, a narrative sung from place to place. Out of these grew a later type of literature called the Puranas (*purana* = the ancient = the story of the past). These, besides the stories of various Kshatriya dynasties, contained cosmogonies and cosmologies and a lot of didactic matter. The narrators of the Puranas were also sutas. The Mahabharata, the Ramayana and the Puranas have been given a special name by a scholar, Dr. S. V. Ketkar, who called these the *sauta* literature, that is, literature belonging to the sutas, preserved and sung by the sutas and perhaps largely composed by the sutas. This literature embodied the secular political tradition of Sanskrit literature as against another branch which he called *mantra*. 'Mantra' in Sanskrit means 'a hymn' or 'a magical formula'. Mantra literature embodied hymns to gods, magical verses (as in the *Rigveda* and *Atharvaveda*), descriptions of ritual and the uses of hymns in ritual in addition to minute details of the various sacrifices (as in the *Yajurveda* and the books called the Brahmanas). There was also philosophical and esoteric discourse (as in the Upanishads and Aranyakas). This literature later branched out into grammar, semantics and philosophy. As against the sauta tradition, this branch represented ritual and religious literature and, later, speculative literature. The traditional keepers of this literature were the people of the priestly class, the *Brahmans*.

It has been convincingly shown by the late Dr. V. S. Sukhtankar that the Mahabharata at a certain point in time went from the sutas into the keeping of a Brahman clan named Bhrigu. This clan took the opportunity to add the stories of its own clan to the Mahabharata. Fortunately, these additions are so crude and so out of context in relation to the original story that they can be detected easily. This author thinks that not only the Mahabharata but almost all the literary tradition in Sanskrit passed into the hands of the Brahmans who henceforth became jealous custodians of this literature to which they added, from time to time, whatever came into their hands. The particular historical and social conditions that made this possible and the time when this occurred would be worth investigating.

The present critical text has eighteen divisions, each called a *parva* or *parvan*. The names of the main parvans and the number of couplets contained in each are as follows:

1. *Adiparva,* 7,982
2. *Sabhaparva,* 2,511
3. *Vana - or Aranyaparva,* 11,664
4. *Virataparva,* 2,500
5. *Udyogaparva,* 6,698
6. *Bhishmaparva,* 5,864
7. *Dronaparva,* 8,909
8. *Karnaparva,* 4,900
9. *Shalyaparva,* 3,220
10. *Sauptikaparva,* 870
11. *Striparva,* 775
12. *Shantiparva,* 14,525
13. *Anushasanaparva,* 6,700
14. *Ashvamedhikaparva,* 3,320
15. *Ashramavasikaparva,* 1,506
16. *Mausalaparva,* 300
17. *Mahaprasthanikaparva,* 120
18. *Svargarohanaparva,* 200

The mode of narration of this book became the standard for some kinds of story literature in Sanskrit, in Ardhamagadhi Jain literature and in Prakrit stories like the *Brihat-Katha.* There are stories within stories, and the thread of the main story is taken up after many such narrations. Sometimes the main story seems almost forgotten or lost but then it is taken up again. Readers of the *Arabian Nights* know this form, which was apparently borrowed from the Indian model. Another feature of this narration is that it is told by many narrators, wherever such opportunities arose, in the words of the actual actors. A story is told as follows — 'In the forest of Naimisha, the Brahman Shaunaka was engaged in performing a ritual which would go on for twelve years, involving many kinds of sacrifices and performances of rites in the mornings and evenings. The afternoons were free. Such a performance needed the help of many priests and also attracted many people who helped to perform it.' It also attracted, among others, story-tellers. Famous among them was the suta story-teller, Lomaharshana (the hair-raiser).

His son Ugrashrava (the loud-voiced) Lomaharshani came along one day and was greeted with cries of joy and implored to tell about his wanderings and also a story. He told of how he had visited many sacred places and of how King Janamejaya of Hastinapura had performed a sacrifice in which all the Nagas were to be sacrificed. This sacrifice was undertaken to avenge his father, King Parikshita, who was killed by a Naga. The terrible slaughter of the Nagas was cleverly stopped by a man named Astika. The sage Vyasa appeared before Janamejaya and persuaded him to give up ideas of revenge. Then Janamejaya expressed a wish to hear the story of the exploits of his ancestors. Vyasa deputed one of his disciples, named Vaishampayana, to tell the story. From this point onwards the story is told as narrated by Vaishampayana to King Janamejaya. When the battle in the Mahabharata started (*Bhishmaparva,* see above), the blind King Dhritarashtra wanted to know what was happening on the battlefield. The eye-witness account of the battle was given to the king by a suta called Sanjaya. This portion is told in the words of Sanjaya.

So we have the first narrator, Ugrashrava, who tells the story up to a point, and then tells it as told by the second narrator, Vaishampayana, who in his turn is the chief narrator up to a point and then tells it as told by the third narrator, Sanjaya, and after the battle portion resumes telling. Besides these three, there are a number of people recounting occasional stories of lesser importance.

* * * * *

The Mahabharata is supposed to have been composed by the sage Vyasa, who played a part in the events and who was an eye-witness of many of them. He is supposed to have told his stories to his disciples. Of these one was Vaishampayana and the other was Jaimini. It is thought that the Vaishampayana version, which is the one before us, differed from the version given by Jaimini. Of this latter version only a fragment apparently remains. As already mentioned above, the original Mahabharata was called *Jaya* and for centuries people have been adding to it, so we have our present Mahabharata. Vyasa is supposed to be *chiranjiva,* a word which can be translated to mean either 'ever-alive', 'an immortal' (which is what he is generally supposed to be) or 'one who lived long' (chira = long, ever; jiva = live) which apparently he did. Indian tradition credits Vyasa with editing and putting into order the hymns of the *Rigveda*, *Atharvaveda* and *Yajurveda*. The word `Vyasa' is a title which means 'arranger, a man who throws together or orders'. From the Mahabharata story we know that his own name was Krishna (the black) Dvaipayana (born on an island). If we take into consideration this tradition, then, perhaps, Vyasa was not the original composer of the story but the man who might have taken it as told by the suta bards and arranged it.

2 The Final Effort

The war in the Mahabharata starts in *Bhishmaparva*. As we read the book, however, we become convinced that this is not so much the beginning of the war as Bhishma's last great effort to stop it. Bhishma's whole life has been a fruitless sacrifice, but these last ten days of his life are the climax of futility and sacrifice. Why should he, who had given up everything that was his by right, have, in his extreme old age, accepted the generalship of the Kaurava army? This question keeps nagging the reader. But as we consider his whole life we must conclude that these last actions were not only in consonance with his life, but were also inevitable.

All human effort is fruitless, all human life ends in frustration — was the Mahabharata written to drive home this lesson? Human toil, expectations, hates, friendships — all seem puny and without substance, like withered leaves eddying in the summer wind. But the people who toiled and dreamed and loved and hated remain unforgettable, their memory constantly searing the heart. While reading the Mahabharata, we see each person going inexorably to a definite end. We become acutely aware that each person knows his end, and his agony and dread become our own. And through the agony of each, we experience the agony of the whole world.

Bhishma's life was full of apparent contradictions, but beneath these contradictions there was a logic in his actions and thought. Bhishma was born a cursed being. His comrades had been freed from the curse by Ganga, but he remained trapped in this world. For some reason Ganga had been forced to live for a time on the earth. At about the same time, Vasishtha had cursed the eight Vasus to be born as mortals. The Vasus came to Ganga and begged of her, 'Let us be born of your womb. Kill us the moment we are born and release us from the world of mortals.' Ganga promised to do so, and the celestial beings set out for the earth. Ganga was a goddess, she had eternal youth; the ordinary rules of earth did not apply to her. This woman descended to the earth, went straight to King Pratipa, sat on his lap and said, 'I want to marry you'. The king replied, 'Lady, if you wanted to marry me you should have sat on my left thigh and not on my right. The right thigh belongs to the son or the daughter-in-law. Let a son be born to me. I will ask him to marry you.' Ganga agreed to this. Pratipa got a son, Shantanu. When this son came of age, Pratipa retired to the forest, leaving the kingdom to him. Shantanu, like other Kshatriyas of his time, was fond of hunting. Once while hunting on the banks of the Ganges he saw a beautiful woman. The hunter was caught! This woman was Ganga. She agreed to marry him, but like other celestial women she laid down peculiar conditions: 'O king, I shall do what I like. I may do things you consider improper, but you must neither prevent nor blame me. The day you do that I will leave you.' The infatuated king agreed to everything and Ganga became his wife. According to the Mahabharata, Ganga gave him every pleasure. But every time a child was born Ganga would take him to the river and drown him. Shantanu was so much in her power that he could not say anything, but when she started to drown the eighth child he could no longer restrain himself. 'At least don't kill this one. What a horrible woman you are!' he exclaimed. That was all the excuse Ganga needed. 'I will spare this child, but according to our agreement I am leaving you.' She vanished and took the child with her.

Both wife and child gone, Shantanu again took to hunting. One day Ganga reappeared to give Shantanu back his son Devavrata, now a youth trained in the arts of the Kshatriyas. Shantanu took him to the capital and made him the crown prince. Devavrata's fine qualities soon endeared him to the people. This being, eager to escape the world, had been trapped as the prince of an ancient house.

Four years passed. Shantanu was as fond of hunting as ever. At this advanced age he once again became the prey of a beautiful woman. This woman was Satyavati, the daughter of Dasharaja, the chieftain of the fisherfolk. This time, not she but her father laid down a condition for marriage. This condition was entirely this-worldly and practical, but because of it Devavrata's life was again given a new direction. 'I will give you my daughter if you promise that her son will inherit the kingdom.' To this Shantanu could not agree. Dejected, he returned to the capital. Devavrata tried to find out what was troubling his father. Shantanu's answer was ambiguous, 'Son, what have I to worry about, with a fine son like you to look after my kingdom? The only thing that concerns me is that you are my only son. If something happens to you, what will become of the kingdom?' The prince went to his father's attendants and found out the whole story. Without telling Shantanu, he went, along with the minister and other courtiers, to Dasharaja and asked for the hand of Satyavati on behalf of his father. When Dasharaja stated his conditions, Devavrata declared before the assembled people, 'I will not claim the kingdom.' Dasharaja, however, was not satisfied with this declaration. 'That is all right. But your children may fight with my daughter's children for the throne.' The prince then took a second vow more difficult than the first, 'I shall remain unmarried for the whole of my life.' Because of this terrible vow, Devavrata was from then on known as Bhishma, 'the Terrible'. Dasharaja was satisfied. He handed his daughter over to Bhishma. 'Mother, come,' with these words Bhishma seated her in a chariot, brought her to the capital, and married her to his father.

Pleased at this extraordinary sacrifice, Shantanu gave Bhishma the power to die when he wished. Long ago, Puru, a prince of the same line, had exchanged his youth for his father's old age, but Puru's sacrifice was only temporary and he was amply rewarded for it. Though Puru was the youngest son, his father disinherited the elder brothers and gave the kingdom to Puru. What did Bhishma get in return for his sacrifice? Death at will! Bhishma's sacrifice had been made with no thought of a return. He himself did not know that he was a cursed being, but Ganga had revealed this secret to Shantanu. Shantanu's gift acquires new significance if we assume that though Bhishma had no memory of his former life he was unconsciously influenced by it. Had this being, trapped in the world he had hoped to escape at birth, taken this opportunity to find release? Unburdened by kingdom and marriage, endowed with the power to die at will, Bhishma was free to leave the world. The caged bird had at last found an escape. But the destiny born with Bhishma once again cast him back into fetters.

Satyavati gave birth to two sons. While they were yet children, Shantanu died. Bhishma could not leave his young step-mother and her young sons; once again he was entangled in the demands of life. Though he was not the king, for over two generations — more than forty years — he took care of the kingdom and wielded authority. Unmarried himself, he had to face all the troubles of finding brides for two generations. The day he brought Satyavati and married her to his father was like a prologue to his later life. In the marriages of Vichitravirya, Dhritarashtra, Pandu and Vidura, it was he who took the initiative. The bachelor who had no children of his own, spent his whole life in caring for other people's children. Right up to the last, he remained entangled.

Satyavati's elder son was put on the throne, but he

died soon after in a quarrel. The second son, Vichitravirya, became king while still very young. Thinking that it would be better to get him married as soon as possible, Bhishma went to the *swayamvara* (ceremony where a bride chooses her husband) of the three princesses of Kashi and abducted all three. When Amba the eldest told him that she had already given her love to Shalva, he sent her to Shalva and had her two younger sisters married to Vichitravirya.

The girls had been brought from Kashi to Hastinapura. There Amba announced her intention to marry Shalva and was sent to him. From the time she had left Kashi until her arrival at Shalva's, some weeks had elapsed. Saying he could not marry a girl who had been so long in the company of another, Shalva sent her back. Amba went to Bhishma and said, 'Since you have abducted me, you must marry me.' Because of his oath of celibacy, Bhishma refused, and finally the slighted, dishonoured, shelterless Amba committed suicide by burning herself. Up to this time Bhishma's life had been blameless, no one had to die cursing him. Amba was the first person he had ever injured. Later there were to be many others.

Vichitravirya died soon after his marriage without leaving any issue. Not only were Satyavati's hopes for her sons ruined, but the whole Kuru line was also threatened with extinction. Pitifully she begged Bishma to give up his vows, accept the throne, and re-establish the line or, if not, at least to beget children by his brother's wives. Bhishma flatly refused. There was one other way. Satyavati had a son, Vyasa, born to her through a Brahman before her marriage to Shantanu. As the half-brother of Vichitravirya he was also the brother-in-law of the queens. Satyavati decided, with Bhishma's consent, to ask him to father sons on behalf of the dead king. She went to the eldest daughter-in-law and said, 'Daughter, tonight prepare to receive your brother-in-law.' Hearing these vague words, the woman waited eagerly, wondering if it was Bhishma or some other Kuru warrior who was coming. Suddenly she was approached by a black, red-eyed man with unkempt hair. She fell unconscious. When the son of that union — Dhritarashtra — was born blind, Satyavati sent Vyasa to the second queen. This woman, seeing his wild appearance, turned white with fear and later gave birth to an albino child. The child was Pandu, 'the White'. These high-born princesses were utterly revolted by the wild ascetic. The third time they heard he was being sent they substituted a maid-servant in the bed. The child born to her was Vidura.

For the blind Dhritarashtra, Bhishma brought a princess from a far-away land. As soon as she heard that her husband was blind, she bandaged her eyes for life. Kunti, stout and no longer young, and the lovely Madri were married to the impotent Pandu. Poor Madri, when still very young, burned herself on her husband's funeral pyre. How all these women must have suffered! How they must have cursed Bhishma! He alone was responsible for their humiliation. Bhishma was the active leader of the Kuru clan, the one who wielded authority. In his zeal to perpetuate his house, he had humiliated and disgraced these royal women. There is no mention of what people felt about Kunti, Madri, or Gandhari, but for his treatment of the princesses of Kashi, Bhishma was strongly denounced by Shishupala. The occasion was a *yajna* (sacrifice) held by Yudhisthira (also known as Dharma). A discussion arose as to who should be honoured as the chief guest. All the great kings had been invited. Each one had to be ritually welcomed. With Bhishma's consent, the Pandavas decided to give the first honour to Krishna. When they started to do so, Shishupala raised an objection: 'Rather than an outsider, you should first honour Bhishma, the eldest in your own family.' This was an unanswerable point, and even Krishna had nothing to say against it. But Bhishma himself rose and tried to show how Krishna was the right choice from all points of view. Then Shishupala lost his temper. 'Bhishma, your whole life is a blot on the name of the Kshatriyas. Though it was known to all that Amba had been promised to Shalva, you abducted her. Your brother being a saintly king did not marry her, so she naturally came to you; but you rejected her. After your brother died his queens were yours by right. Instead, you had a Brahman secretly father their children. You are not celibate, you are just impotent! And now, when it is proper that you should receive the first honour, you stand there singing Krishna's praises!'

Fortunately, Bhishma did not have to find brides for Duryodhana and Dharma. In that generation, no woman suffered because of his doing. But in the court where he sat as the eldest, he did not lift a finger to halt the indignity to a woman. When Draupadi was dragged into the court of Dhritarashtra, Vidura was the one to intervene. Vidura had no power. He was the younger brother of Dhritarashtra! Besides, he was the son of a slave. Bhishma, on the other hand, had the authority to stop the shameful spectacle. Instead, he sat there futilely discussing what was *dharma* [1] and what was not dharma.

The Mahabharata does not reveal that there was any attitude of chivalry towards women. But no man had shown the utter callousness that Bhishma had. Yet, we cannot say that Bhishma committed all this cruelty deliberately. It seems that he was indifferent to it. Did this indifference arise out of his obsession with one goal — the perpetuation of the Kuru line? He had sacrificed himself completely. He no longer lived for himself. Could that excuse his almost inhuman treatment of these women? Is a person justified in doing things for others which would be condemned if he did them for himself? Or does the Mahabharata want to emphasize that human life, whether lived for oneself or spent in unselfish endeavour, must inevitably result in wrong to others?

Or, in this life of self-sacrifice, was the self still lurking somewhere? Why did Bhishma consent to having Vyasa beget the children? From the account in the Mahabharata it would appear that there were enough young men at the court of the Kurus. If such a man had been chosen to father the children he might have gained some position at the Kuru court. Was Bhishma afraid

---

1 Dharma is a word which has many meanings. Here it can be taken to mean 'right'.

that this might jeopardize his authority? In Bhishma's horoscope there were no stars for kingship, but certainly there were many for great authority over a long period. Choosing Vyasa helped Bhishma to retain his authority and at the same time to remain true to his vow. However justifiable his actions may have been in the realm of politics, they are certainly blameworthy from the human point of view.

In his tirade against Bhishma, Shishupala had called him *prajnamanin* (considering himself wise). It was true. Bhishma was famed as a man completely unselfish, wise, true to his word — as a man who lived for the good of his clan, not himself. And Bhishma was trying his utmost to live up to this role. When a man does something for himself his actions are performed within certain limits — limits set by the jealous scrutiny of others. But let a man set out to sacrifice himself and do good to others, and the normal limits vanish. He can become completely ruthless in carrying out his objectives. The injustices done by idealists, patriots, saints and crusaders are far greater than those done by the worst tyrants. Had Bhishma, too, become intoxicated by his own public image? No, we cannot say that he ever got so carried away that he forgot what he was. But having publicly assumed his difficult role and unnecessarily undertaken great responsibilities, he had to play his part to the end.

After Duryodhana grew up Bhishma no longer wielded power. He was an honoured old man at the court of the Kurus. But even in the matter of honour he had to step back. At the time of Dharma's yajna,

Shishupala was right — the honour of the first place belonged to Bhishma. It was, however, conferred on Krishna. His authority gone, his status diminished, Bhishma could well have retired. Before the great war, Vyasa came to the Kuru court and said to his mother Satyavati, 'I see great destruction. Take your two daughters-in-law and retire to the forest.' Satyavati and the women went to the forest to die. Bhishma was older than his step-mother. He could also have taken this way out. Why did he remain at the court? Why did he later accept the generalship of the Kaurava army?

One can hardly say he was a great warrior. He had the reputation of being one, he also considered himself one. But he never fought a great battle during his own long life. The abduction of the Kashi princesses showed audacity and planning, but as far as we can see from the Mahabharata it involved no fighting. The one incident on which his reputation as a warrior rests, and which is referred to again and again in the Mahabharata, is his three weeks' combat with Parashurama. An analysis of the incident, however, shows that it could not have been true. Parashurama, the killer of the Haihayas, is supposed to have lived in the first *yuga* (epoch) of the world. After him came Rama of Ayodhya, years after whose death the Mahabharata story is supposed to have taken place. So Parashurama as a hero belongs to an epoch long past. Moreover, this story belongs to a whole series of stories about people of the Bhrigu clan, which scholars agree are later interpolations.

After Pandu became king he is reported to have gone on a tour of conquest. Bhishma never accompanied him; he stayed back in Hastinapura. In his old age, he joined a party raiding the cattle of Virata. The Mahabharata describes vividly how Arjuna routed all the Kaurava raiders, including Bhishma.

Bhishma obviously was no great warrior. Besides, at the time he took up the generalship he was an extremely old man. At the very least, he must have been between ninety and one hundred years old. We can calculate his age in the following way: When Bhishma's father married Satyavati, Bhishma was the crown prince. He had already been trained in archery, so he must have been *at least* sixteen. After his first step-brother was killed in a fight, his younger brother came to the throne and married. If we take it for granted that Vichitravirya was at least sixteen at that time and that he was born to Satyavati two years after her marriage, then Bhishma must have been thirty-four. Immediately after his marriage, Vichitravirya died. Then, on the widows and the maidservant of Vichitravirya, Vyasa fathered three sons: Dhritarashtra, Pandu and Vidura. From the death of Vichitravirya to the birth of Pandu, at least two years must have elapsed, so at that time Bhishma must have been thirty-six. Assuming that Pandu also ascended the throne and married at sixteen, then at the time of Pandu's coronation Bhishma was fifty-two. Without taking into account the stories of Pandu's tour of conquest, if we assume that Dharma, Bhima and Arjuna were born one after the other soon after Pandu's marriage, Bhishma's age would be fifty-five at the birth of Arjuna.

From all the exploits Arjuna performed before his

marriage, it would appear that he was above sixteen. But even granting that he was only sixteen, Bhishma must have been seventy-one at the time of Draupadi's swayamvara. After the swayamvara the Pandavas went to Indraprastha, and shortly after their arrival there, Arjuna was sent into exile. Near the end of his exile he went to Dvaraka, married Subhadra and returned to Indraprastha, where his son Abhimanyu was born. According to the Mahabharata, this exile lasted for twelve years. Taking for granted that this is an exaggeration and the exile lasted only twelve months, Arjuna was eighteen at the time of his son's birth. From this time onwards a large number of events took place before the Pandavas went into exile: the burning of the Khandava forest, the building of the Mayasabha palace, Dharma's great yajna, the disastrous dice game. These events must have taken at least three years. The next thirteen years were spent in exile, at the close of which Abhimanyu was married. That means that at this time Abhimanyu was sixteen, Arjuna was thirty-four and Bhishma was eighty-nine. If we allow just one year between this time and the beginning of the battle, then Bhishma was ninety years old when the battle was fought. The Mahabharata calls him 'the grandfather' and 'the oldest among the Kurus'. His acceptance of the generalship in his extreme old age seems to be entirely incongruous with everything we know about him.

At the very beginning of his life Bhishma had sacrificed whatever was for himself. But at the same time the great responsibilities of protecting the clan had fallen on his shoulders. He did not have to fight battles, but he had to order the lives of two generations. He brought up other people's children, found brides for all, including the blind and the impotent. His labour bore fruit in that for the first time in three generations healthy young children filled the palace of Hastinapura. It was Bhishma who looked after their welfare, who had them educated and trained in the arts of Kshatriyahood. As the princes grew older, however, his hold on authority loosened. He had no hand in their marriages, nor could he stop their quarrels. He had discharged his duties and could now have retired honourably to the forest. That is what a Kshatriya was supposed to do. A man was severely criticized if he refused to relinquish power after his children were married and had children of their own. But this rule applied to ordinary family men immersed in their own affairs. Did Bhishma think that he was immune because he belonged to that category of men who sacrifice the self and live only for others? Did he feel, as such people do, that he could never give up his responsibilities but must die in harness? All duties ended, with a boon allowing him to die at will in his possession, he could have escaped the world. But he would not.

He *would* not. During the first part of his life circumstances had forced him into deeper and deeper involvements with the affairs of his family. He had no choice; he had to fulfil the duties thrust upon him. But in this last chapter of his life it looks as if he had deliberately sought out responsibilities that were not even his.

But did he have a choice after all? Having taken up a life-long burden, he could not lay it down at any time. He had tried again and again to bring peace among the warring cousins whose rivalries were to ruin the clan once again. His decision was inevitable. And the pains he might have suffered in keeping his vows were nothing in comparison to the humiliation and agony of his last ten days.

Duryodhana came to Bhishma and said to him, 'Sir, you are the eldest among us, you are a famous warrior. Be our general and lead us.' Duryodhana's offer was a formality, paying Bhishma the honour which had been denied to him by the Pandavas at the sacrifice. Duryodhana fully expected Bhishma to refuse. But to the astonishment of all, Bhishma promptly accepted. He went further. He deliberately insulted Karna, the chief warrior on the Kaurava side and an arch-enemy of the Pandavas. Karna vowed to keep away from the battle as long as Bhishma lived.

Bhishma had thus set aside the person he thought was the chief obstacle to his efforts at peace. Further, by his acceptance of the post, Bhishma had deliberately created a dilemma for both parties. Duryodhana could not pursue the war with the vigour he wanted. On the other side, since Bhishma was the eldest of the clan and the grandfather of the fighting warriors, it was impossible for the Pandavas to kill him. The greatest warrior of the Pandavas was Arjuna, and he was the very one for whom the killing of Bhishma was an impossibility. The *Bhagavadgita* opens with Arjuna's

'How can I in battle send arrows against Bhishma, against Drona, at whose feet I must ever bow in respect?' That was the anguish of Arjuna's heart. Later Arjuna again recalled how as a small boy he had sat in Bhishma's lap and called him father, and how Bhishma had told him, 'Little one, I am your grandfather, not your father.' Bhishma was absolutely right in his calculations. He was invulnerable, not because he was immortal, nor because he was a great warrior, but because he was the Pandavas' grandfather. The whole of the Gita in which Krishna tried to persuade Arjuna to stand up and fight proved fruitless as far as the killing of Bhishma was concerned.

But Bhishma forgot to take into consideration the families related by marriage. His body was inviolate to the Pandavas, but certainly not to Draupadi's brothers. Amba had been reborn as Shikhandi, the eldest brother of Draupadi, for the sole purpose of killing Bhishma. Draupadi's brother, Dhrishtadyumna, who had emerged with her out of the fire, had been born to kill Drona. Both fulfilled their appointed tasks.

Krishna tried his utmost to get Arjuna to kill Bhishma, but when he saw that Arjuna's heart was not in the fight against the old man, he threw down the reins, jumped out of the chariot, and rushed towards Bhishma. The Mahabharata recounts this incident twice — on the third day and on the ninth. The incident on the third day is an obvious later interpolation. On the ninth day, Krishna rushed towards Bhishma with the whip in his hand. Arjuna ran after Krishna, held him tightly by the feet, and beseeched him to come back to the chariot. Arjuna still refused to kill Bhishma, but at last, with extreme reluctance, he promised to knock him out of his chariot. As the general of a great army, and reputedly a great warrior, Bhishma wanted the glory of being killed by the greatest warrior of his day, namely Arjuna. And this was exactly what Arjuna did not want. At last, after a monotonous ding-dong battle of nine days, Arjuna had to confer that honour on Bhishma. He had to stand with Shikhandi and shower arrows on the old general. He had to give an opportunity for Bhishma to say, 'Those horrible sharp arrows cutting at my heart cannot be Shikhandi's, they must be Arjuna's.'

The whole of the Mahabharata battle is said to have lasted for eighteen days, but the real carnage came only after Bhishma's fall. The first ten days, when Bhishma was the general, were only a make-believe war. Bhishma was making his last desperate attempt to stop the fratricidal conflict. Almost every day Bhishma tried to persuade Duryodhana to stop the war. But even at the price of his life he could not. Bhishma's intentions become very clear in the Mahabharata's day-to-day account of the fighting.

First day: Seeing the vast army of the Kauravas, Dharma becomes discouraged. Arjuna urges him to take heart but he himself, when facing Bhishma and Drona, has no spirit for the fight. Krishna pours out the whole Gita in an effort to give him courage. Dharma goes into the Kaurava camp to pay his respects to Bhishma and Drona. Yuyutsu, a step-brother of Duryodhana, joins the Pandavas. There is a great fight,

Uttar, the prince of Virata, is killed. The first day's victory goes to the Kauravas.

Second day: Fights between Bhishma and Arjuna, Drona and Dhrishtadyumna, etc. On the Kaurava side the king of Kalinga and his son are killed. The day goes well for the Pandavas.

Third day: Duryodhana is knocked unconscious by Bhima and is taken away from the battlefield by his charioteer. The Kaurava army is in disarray. Meanwhile, Duryodhana recovers and regroups his forces. He censures Bhishma for his conduct of the war. Bhishma answers that the Pandavas are invincible, but he promises to do his best. Bhishma fights bravely. Krishna leaps from his chariot, his discus in hand, and rushes on Bhishma. Arjuna brings him back. On the whole, the day is the Pandavas'.

Fourth day: Great fights. Day's honours to the Pandavas. At night Duryodhana again berates Bhishma for his slackness. Bhishma contends that Arjuna and Krishna are godlike and cannot be defeated. He advises Duryodhana to stop the war.

Fifth day: Fights as usual. No great victory to either side.

Sixth day: Like the fifth.

Seventh day: At the very beginning of the day, Duryodhana upbraids Bhishma. Bhishma gives his fixed answer, 'The Pandavas are invincible, but I will try my best.' A great fight. Dharma assails Shikhandi, 'Why have you not killed Bhishma?'

Eighth day: On the Kaurava side the sons of Shakuni are killed. A dozen of Duryodhana's brothers are also killed. On the Pandava side Iravata dies. The fight goes on right up to sundown. That night a council of war is held by Duryodhana, Duhshasana, Shakuni and Karna. Karna advises Duryodhana to remove Bhishma from the generalship. Duryodhana goes with his brother to Bhishma and gives him an ultimatum. Once again Bhishma reiterates his plea about the Pandavas' invincibility, but promises to do his best.

Ninth day: Bhishma fights valiantly. Seeing that Arjuna is powerless against the old man, Krishna leaps from his chariot and rushes towards Bhishma with his whip in his hand. Arjuna brings him back. The battle stops. The day goes well for the Kauravas. At night the Pandavas go to Bhishma and ask how he can be killed. He advises them to have Shikhandi fight him. Meanwhile, Krishna beseeches Arjuna, 'If you will not kill Bhishma, at least make him fall from the chariot.' Arjuna agrees with great reluctance and shame.

Tenth day: Shikhandi showers arrows on Bhishma. Behind him stands Arjuna, also shooting arrows at the old general. Arjuna's arrows pierce Bhishma's armour. One arrow hits Bhishma on the head. The blow throws Bhishma out of his chariot and he falls on a thick layer of arrows without his body touching the earth. All this time Bhishma is accompanied by Duhshasana to whom he is speaking right up to the last.

The battle stops temporarily after the fall of Bhishma. The warriors on both sides come to pay their respects to the wounded hero. Bhishma requests Duryodhana, 'Let your feud with the Pandavas end with my death. Make a treaty with them.' Karna comes alone to pay his respects. Bhishma advises him to join the Pandavas but Karna refuses.

In this account of the ten days' fighting there are some striking inconsistencies. The story of Shikhandi's birth must have been known to Dharma. Everyone had noticed that Bhishma would not fight Shikhandi. On the seventh day Dharma had abused Shikhandi for not killing Bhishma. Under the circumstances it seems ridiculous that Dharma felt the necessity to ask Bhishma how he could be killed. Apparently, this last incident appears to have been invented to perpetuate the myth of Bhishma's invulnerability.

Krishna's leaping from the chariot, discus in hand, on the third day also does not fit. The whole incident is described in a very poetic and exaggerated fashion, with a lengthy description of Krishna's divinity. Krishna with the discus in his hand is the traditional picture of the divine Krishna. It is queer that this divine manifestation of Krishna had no effect on Arjuna. On the other hand, the incident of the ninth day, in which Krishna leaped down with a whip in his hand, has all the stamp of authenticity. Krishna was driving the chariot of Arjuna. That he should leap with his whip in his hand seems natural. The whole description of the incident is in the usual style of the Mahabharata, concise and unexaggerated. Moreover, it fits in the chain of events which leads to the climax of the tenth day.

The third incongruity is in the description of Bhishma's fight. When a charioteer fought another charioteer, it was not just two people shooting at one another. It was a very elaborate fight. For example, we are told that Yudhamanyu was protecting Arjuna's left wheel, Uttamauja was guarding the right wheel, and Arjuna himself was guarding Shikhandi from the back. In the same way, Duryodhana had ordered that all should endeavour to protect Bhishma. He had told his brother Duhshasana, 'Have chariots on all sides to protect him. You should have but two objectives: the protection of Bhishma and the killing of Shikhandi.' We are told that Duryodhana's own sons were guarding Bhishma from behind and that kings of different countries were protecting him on both sides. It was not as if Shikhandi and Arjuna were shooting arrows at an unprotected Bhishma.

But in the last day's description we are not told who was protecting Bhishma. We only hear Bhishma describing to Duhshasana how he is being hurt by Arjuna's arrows. Duhshasana had been especially appointed to guard Bhishma. What was he doing at that time? Was everyone so exasperated that they wanted Bhishma out of the way?

Even at the end Bhishma's fate pursued him. He did not die by Arjuna's arrows. He only fell down wounded. Now he could have used his father's gift and found release. But the sun was in the south; dying souls could find no rest. Bhishma had to use his blessing to prolong his death for six more months. For six months Bhishma's body lay immobilized, but his eyes could see, and with them he had to watch the carnage of the Kuru clan. He could hear, and with his ears he had to hear the laments of the widowed Kuru women. He could talk. And with his lips, later authors made him speak the banalities of *Shantiparva*.

Had Bhishma accomplished anything in keeping his vows? The question remains.

3 Gandhari*

1

The hilly country had ended. They had reached the vast, monotonous plain of northern India. Now only rivers or occasional forests obstructed their progress. Most of the time the princess rode in a chariot, or was carried in a palanquin; sometimes she walked. Her companion was a maid slightly older than herself. When they were leaving, it was she who had consoled the princess. By pointing out beautiful spots on the way and telling her amusing stories, she tried to keep Gandhari's spirits up. From her father's house, only Gandhari's brother Shakuni accompanied her. He, too, looked after the comfort of his sister. Gradually, thoughts of the land of Gandhara receded and Gandhari's mind became absorbed in painting pictures of the unseen Hastinapura. When the people from Hastinapura had come to ask for her hand, their gifts had dazzled everyone. Their chariots, their clothing, their ornaments

---

* The critical edition does not have most things said in this sketch. It has only the following about Gandhari: (1) She bound her eyes with cloth when she heard that her husband to be was born blind. (2) Gandhari gave birth to many children. All the sons died at the hands of the Pandavas in the battle. (3) Dhritarashtra, Gandhari and Kunti died in a forest fire. Vidura had died before them.

were rich and splendid. Their behaviour and speech were urbane. Already her retinue was made up almost entirely of these people; there was almost no one from Gandhara. Their journey was so long and so fast that the princess was fatigued both in mind and body. Finally, she longed only for the journey to end.

At last it was over. Bhishma came out of the city to greet the Gandhara princess. As her retinue rode through the city, people stood on both sides to welcome her. But Gandhari was too tired to pay any attention to them. She went immediately to the chambers reserved for her. For two days she remained there, exhausted and listless. But every day her companion would go about the palace and return with new descriptions of the splendour of the Kurus. Gandhari was astounded to hear that her brother Shakuni, the prince of Gandhara, had decided to stay on permanently in Hastinapura. However, she knew of many cases where a man whose elder brother was on the throne had gone to another kingdom to obtain wealth and fortune. It was good to think that although she had come so far, she was not completely cut off from her home. When her companion described Shakuni's palace, she felt proud of the wealth of her husband's people. By evening she ceased to think of her own home and became absorbed in the crowded capital below and the broad forests beyond, along the banks of the Yamuna. In Gandhara she had never seen such a vast expanse of level land. This palace too was much bigger than that of her parents. Gradually, she ceased to think of her own home and became absorbed in the thoughts of being queen in this splendid house. Just then her friend came in. 'Today what will she tell me about their grandeur?' Gandhari looked at her expectantly. But today the girl looked different. She did not come in as usual, animated and gay. Her face was white, her steps faltered. Thinking her friend must be sick, she stepped towards her. Her friend came up to her with great effort, gripped the princess' hands, and burst out, 'You are betrayed, poor darling, we are betrayed. The prince you are going to marry is blind from birth.' For a moment, Gandhari did not comprehend her friend's words. The next moment she fell to the floor unconscious.

* * * * *

2

Gandhari was seated in her palace. Her companion was standing behind her, gently stroking Gandhari's hair. 'Take courage, princess.' Though Gandhari was now not only a mother but a grandmother, her friend still used her childhood title, 'Princess'. As soon as she had said these words her friend thought to herself, 'How foolishly do I talk! What hope has this poor woman left? Though the rest of her sons were gone, as long as Duryodhana was alive, she still had a son. She could master her grief and hold her head up. What can she do now?' Aloud she said, 'Calm yourself, Gandhari.' Gandhari sighed and answered, 'There is nothing that can upset me now. After I had many children you thought that your Gandhari would at least be happy. But it was never so. If they were hurt, my heart would start to pound; if I heard them crying, I used to grieve and get flurried. If I heard that they didn't win in the chariot race, I would get dejected. The day they came back humiliated from the ill-fated trip for inspecting the royal herds, I felt sadder than they themselves. When the Pandavas were being sent to a small town on the border, those helpless children came to say farewell. Outwardly I gave them my blessing, but in my heart I was thinking, "Good, now my children's way is clear". Before the war, it was only at your urging that I went into the assembly and advised them not to fight. Inwardly I was telling myself that if they fought, the kingship of Hastinapura would remain with my sons. Later, after the war started, I faced each new day with the dread, "What will be the news today?" Then as the battle went against them I would ask myself, "Today how many are left?" Each child was a new sorrow. I had no life of my own. All my life, their moments of happiness were my moments of happiness, their moments of sorrow were mine.' As she spoke, Gandhari's voice grew louder and louder. Her friend looked at her with consternation and pity, 'Be calm, be calm, my sweet'. Immediately Gandhari answered, 'That is what I am telling you. Today I have become completely calm. Now no one's success can make my heart blossom in happiness; no one's defeat can wither it with sorrow. Now there is nobody for whom I can be anxious. My mind is now permanently at peace. There is nothing to hope for, nothing to fear.'

Meanwhile, controlling his own grief, Dhritarashtra had taken the hand of an attendant and come to console Gandhari. From the door he called, 'Gandhari, Gandhari'.

Just as she finished her last sentence, Gandhari heard his call. Immediately she realized how false her words were. As long as her blind husband was alive, she could not escape being subjected to happiness and grief. Agitated, she got to her feet. 'But he—', she managed to utter. For the second time in her life she fell over in a faint. Seeing that the queen had fallen, all the servants hurried towards her. Dhritarashtra's attendant too released the king's hand and rushed towards Gandhari. Dhritarashtra stood alone just inside the door-way. He could hear the confusion around him, but he could not understand what had happened. He stood looking everywhere with his sightless eyes, asking piteously, 'What has happened, what has happened?'

* * * * *

3

Today everyone left the foot of the Himalaya and started up the mountain. In this lower hut there had been servants to wait on them. There were huts of ascetics nearby. Dharma and the other princes had come to visit them twice. On the whole, the tempo of their life was even and quiet. One after another, the days passed for Dhritarashtra and Gandhari, Vidura and Kunti. Vidura, Dhritarashtra and the ascetics would spend their time discussing one subject or another. Gandhari and Kunti would sit listening. Every time visitors came, the outwardly calm stream of their life was disturbed. The whole place became crowded with the retinue of the princes—now kings. As the sons put their heads on the feet of the elders, each one's heart filled with different emotions. After they left, outwardly, all became peaceful, but it took a longer time to quiet the inner turmoil. Today, too, the princes and their wives had come from Hastinapura. Dhritarashtra had made up his mind about something, and said to Dharma, 'Yudhishthira, this is not truly the last *ashrama*. Now let the four of us build a hut and live by ourselves. It has taken us many months to get used to living out here, away from the palace. But now it would be better if we went higher and lived in the forest.' Yudhishthira and the others tried to dissuade him, but Dhritarashtra would not listen. Dharma looked at Vidura. But today Vidura too supported Dhritarashtra. 'Dharma, what Dhritarashtra is saying is right. You must now bid us farewell. You, who know dharma so well, why are you trying to tempt us back into this world? You should also not cling to us.' Kunti's eyes filled up, but she too announced her decision to leave the present hut. Nobody asked Gandhari for her opinion. Everyone assumed that her husband's wish was hers.

The party walked all day. Not only the young men and their wives but the ascetics also accompanied the old people. As they went up, the valley became narrow; the river now was far below them. Finally, Vidura selected an open, quiet, shaded place. There the servants erected a hut and left enough provisions for ten or fifteen days. That night the whole party slept there and in the morning all but the four departed with heavy hearts. Dhritarashtra would not allow a single servant to remain. Vidura promised to take care of

Dhritarashtra's needs and Kunti said that if her sister-in-law consented, she would be happy to look after Gandhari. Gandhari gave her heartfelt consent. 'I do not want a servant,' she said emphatically. Finally the farewells were said. As they were going, Dharma called Vidura aside and told him, 'I am having four or five trusted servants put up a hut and stay about a half mile below. Every few days they will come and look to your needs. Don't refuse them. I am telling them that at other times they should not come near you.' Vidura accompanied the children a short distance and then turned back. Now only the four remained in that lonely place.

After the morning's tasks in the hut were completed, Vidura took Dhritarashtra's hand, and Kunti led Gandhari to a cool, shaded spot. They seated the blind couple, then sat down themselves a little behind. Gandhari was sitting quietly. She let out a deep sigh. Dhritarashtra turned his face toward her and said a little scornfully, 'What's the use of sighing now? Our life has been just what two blind people could expect.' His words and his tone startled Gandhari. She would not normally have replied back but the scorn in his words pricked her. She answered a little drily, 'I wasn't sighing for my sorrow, Your Majesty. Since we came here, the mountain breeze, the thick carpet of needles underfoot, the light smell of the pines, the sighing of the forest in the breeze, and the constant murmuring of the river, all have reminded me of Gandhara; and without realizing it, I sighed. That is all.' At her words, Dhritarashtra lost all desire to hurt her. He said with pity, 'Really, Gandhari, your life was ruined by being bound to a blind man, wasn't it? All your life you must have yearned for your parents' home.' Gandhari answered, 'Not at all. The day I married you I suppressed all thoughts of my parents' home. Today I was recalling the country of Gandhara, not the people. Your Majesty knows that though I lived in the same courtyard as my brother, I never spoke to him.' Several moments went by in silence. Vidura and Kunti sat with astonished expressions. Kunti looked as if she was worrying about the trend of the couple's conversation. It was now Dhritarashtra's turn to speak. The scorn was gone from his voice. Almost pleadingly he said, 'You were deceived. Without being told of my blindness you were married to me. We did you a thousand wrongs, Gandhari. But you have paid them back. Can't you ever forgive and forget?'

Thinking that such a conversation should not be overheard by a third party, Vidura and Kunti rose silently and started to leave. But the blind Dhritarashtra's ear was quicker than the ordinary man's eye. Turning towards Vidura and Kunti, he said, 'Wait, don't go. Sit here. So far in our relationship as husband and wife nothing has taken place in private. There is no reason for any privacy now. As your elder I order you to stay.' As soon as he heard the two sit down, he turned again to Gandhari and said in a choked but excited voice, 'Really, you have punished me severely, Gandhari. I didn't think so at first; at the wedding ritual when you stood with your eyes bound, I did not take it too seriously. I thought that I would plead with you and be able to extinguish your anger with my love. But that was not to be. At night when you came to the bedchamber, your eyes were still bound, and you came stumbling, clutching someone's hand. I was born blind. I had become used to moving about without seeing. But you had deliberately covered your eyes. Your body was not used to blindness. What a horrible night! I don't know why I didn't kill you right then.' Gandhari too retorted bitterly, 'I wish you had. At least we would have avoided this horrible future.' 'Don't talk like that, Gandhari,' Dhritarashtra said passionately. 'No matter how weak we Kuru men have become, we still are Kshatriyas. We don't show our manhood by killing women.' Then he went on as if he had not been interrupted, 'I was king. I could have torn off that blindfold. But I thought that instead of forcing you with my authority, I would persuade you in time. But your first day's resentment became permanent. When you had children, I thought of saying, "Gandhari, if not for me, at least to see the face of your child unbind your eyes." But by that time my heart too had hardened. Perhaps you would have done it for the children, but I was not ready to give you the chance. I had a kind of revengeful pleasure in knowing that you would never see the face of your son. Going around with your eyes bound, you were playing the part of a devoted wife. You were chained by the results of your own actions. Never again could you open your eyes of your own accord. You could only have done it by my order. And that I would not give.

'Through love for our children — blind love though

it was — we came close. Until that time you never felt that I belonged to you. We Kuru men have done great injustices to women. And we have paid in full for them too. In Amba's wrath Bhishma was burned. I am still burning in yours. My children too have been destroyed in it. Kunti also was married to a deficient man. But at least she fulfilled the role of a faithful, if not a very beloved wife during her husband's life. After his death, she constantly guarded the welfare of her children. Every person gets entangled in a mesh of injustices. I wronged you. Pandu wronged Kunti. And whose wrong doing was it that Pandu and I should lead such fruitless lives? Can we say that the wrongs done to our mothers, the misery they suffered, brought this curse on us? Poor Vidura was the only one completely sound in mind and body. He was the son of the same father as we were. But because his mother was a servant, he could not become king. He did not try to take revenge on anyone for his life's disappointment. Kunti and Vidura were the only two people in our whole clan who were consciously watchful. You feel, Gandhari, that you have been cheated and deceived, but think for a moment: in the three generations of our family every person has been cheated and deceived. I am pleading with you not merely to ask for forgiveness, but to persuade you to give up your fight against life. Give up your anger, not only against me, but against life itself. My injustice to you does not give you the right to do an injustice to your children, to your whole life. How can one wrong compensate another, Gandhari? At least now take off that blindfold. Learn to look at the world, at human beings, and at your own past life objectively. Our life is nearly over. At least do not die with your eyes bound.' Dhritarashtra could not speak any more. The others too were immersed in the thoughts he had stirred. After a long while Gandhari said softly, 'Your Majesty, I have uncovered my eyes, but I still can't see clearly.' For the first time in his life Dhritarashtra gripped her hand hard and cried like a child. In the Kuru clan, Dhritarashtra and Gandhari were the participants of joys and sorrows; Vidura and Kunti were merely witnesses. But today the witnesses also became involved and their eyes were filled with tears. After his emotion had subsided, Dhritarashtra said gently, 'Gandhari, in a day or so, with Kunti's help, you will learn to see. The day you can see clearly, take me by the hand and seat me here.' No one could speak any more. After returning to the hut too, each one was absorbed in his own thoughts.

Two days went by. Gandhari had learned to get about using her eyes. Taking the king's hand, she led him to his usual seat. Again everyone sat down, and as if the two days had not intervened, their conversation continued. Dhritarashtra kept Gandhari's hand in his. He began to speak, 'Gandhari, you are younger than I am. When I am gone, you will be able to manage by yourself now.' Hearing these words, Gandhari put her hand on his lips. 'Never, Your Majesty, that will never happen. I did not hold your hand in order to let it go again. I have opened my eyes not merely for myself but for both of us.' Again Dhritarashtra could not speak. After a long time he quieted his mind and said,

'Gandhari, I can smell and hear what you cannot see. Look, there is a forest fire somewhere. Since morning I have been smelling smoke. I have been hearing the cries of frightened animals. I think that somewhere on this side of the river, behind us, the forest is on fire. It is not yet close enough to feel the heat. Look and see.' Vidura, Kunti and Gandhari rose and looked. Yes, in the distance they began to see smoke. They saw reddish, yellowish tongues of flame moving. All three sat down again. Gandhari said softly but clearly, 'Your Majesty is right. The fire is not even a half mile away.' Dhritarashtra said, 'It will be harder than you thought to hold my hand till the end. I am tired of living here waiting for death, of having the children visit us every five or six months, stirring up old griefs, so that I have to quiet my mind all over again. You can cross the river and escape from the fire.' Gandhari gripped Dhritarashtra's hand more firmly, 'Your Majesty, now I am not going to leave you. Come, instead of waiting for the fire, let us walk towards it.'

'You are right, Gandhari.' Dhritarashtra stood up. He and Gandhari started forward. Hearing Vidura and Kunti coming behind them, he stopped, 'You too—' That was all he said. Again he turned and started forward.

An extraordinary thing was happening. A *sati* was holding her living husband's hand and walking to the pyre. Instead of lifting his dead brother's widow from the flames, a brother-in-law (Vidura) was walking to the fire with her.

4 Kunti

It is on extremely rare occasions that one feels one has been able to shape one's life even to a small extent. Most often the feeling is that of floating directionless like a sere leaf in the wind. The making of some lives is entirely in the hands of others. That was the case of women in the times of the Mahabharata. Their happiness, their sorrows were decreed by men to whom they belonged. Men acted, men directed and women suffered. Gandhari, Draupadi, Subhadra, were such women but they were given at least a few years of wealth and well-being. Married to a blind man, Gandhari was virtually a queen in Hastinapura, though her husband was never crowned king; and when her son ruled, she was the queen-mother. Draupadi drank deep of sorrow but lived long as the queen and wife of the conquering heroes. Subhadra never became the chief queen, but lived in wealth, saw her son's son crowned king and became the guardian of the two young kings: her own grandson and the grandson of her brother Krishna. Kunti alone among them seems to have been born to endure only sorrow. A dozen years of happiness were too few to compensate her for her long life of sorrow and humiliations. Every man in her life contributed to her unhappiness. She never said anything directly blaming her husband, but she did reproach her father bitterly: 'As a spendthrift squanders his money unthinking, so did my father give me away when yet a girl to his friend.'[1] Though one feels pity for her, in her own estimate her condition, sometimes full of sorrow, was never lowly or pitiable. She did not think that ease or riches were necessary for the happiness of a Kshatriya woman. She again and again gave expression to what she thought was the glory of a Kshatriya woman. She felt that she had behaved according to the Kshatriya mores and had won the consequent rewards.

Kunti's father was a Yadava prince called Shurasena. He had a very dear friend and cousin called Kuntibhoja.[2] This friend was childless. It was customary in those times for heirless kings to seek the favour and blessings of a Brahman in order to get a son. The chosen Brahman would be a guest in the palace, fed and waited upon by the daughter of the house. Since Kuntibhoja hadn't even a daughter, he asked his friend Shurasena for the gift of Kunti, and Shurasena gave her away. Kunti's own name was Pritha. It shows that she was apparently a large, big-boned girl. She was better known as Kunti, which means 'a princess of the kingdom of Kunti'.

The adoptive father employed Kunti to serve and

---

1 This passage might be a later interpolation because the relative ages of Kunti and Krishna implied in that speech go counter to the other evidence in the story.

2 Kunti was the name of the country. Bhoja denoted the king of a dependent position as a chieftain who paid tribute to a bigger king.

win the favour of a Brahman sage called Durvasa, who was famous for his magical powers as well as his bad temper. Service in this context meant personal service: being at the beck and call of the sage, doing his bidding, even sharing his bed if he so desired. The sage was so well served by her that he went away pleased. He promised progeny to the king and gave Kunti some mantras (magic formulae) by which she could compel any god to beget sons upon her. She was full of curiosity and recited one mantra to see what would happen. It was the mantra calling the Sun-god, who came, and she conceived a son. Kunti's old nurse kept the whole affair a secret and when the baby was born, she put him in a box along with a lot of gold and floated the box on a small river. This child of Kunti's was supposed to be born with *kundalas* (ear ornaments) and *kavacha* (armour). The Mahabharata records many miraculous events, some of which seem to be later additions made to explain away the human weaknesses displayed by those heroic people. There are others which cannot be so easily accounted for. A son being born to Kunti from the Sun-god falls in the first category. Kunti was serving a Brahman for a year and that she should bear him a son was not such an extraordinary occurrence.[1] The fact that Kunti's old nurse helped to dispose of the boy and that a lot of gold was kept with him lends support to the supposition that this eventuality was

1 There is a record in the Mahabharata itself of another woman, Satyavati, Kunti's grandmother-in-law, having had a child before marriage by a Brahman.

foreseen and provided for by her adoptive father when he gave her to the Brahman. What one cannot understand is why the Sun-god was said to have fathered the boy. This god plays a very subordinate and sorry part throughout the later narrative. (See ch.9.) The ear ornaments and the armour belong to the second category of miracles. They are neither easy to explain nor to understand. Another story in the Mahabharata suggests that they might have been the signs of Kshatriyahood. They are called *sahaja* ('born with' a person), maybe because a Kshatriya is born with the right to wear them. This boy was found by a man of the suta caste. Because he was found with a lot of wealth he was named Vasusena, the wealthy one. The name-ending 'sena' was definitely that of a Kshatriya. This strengthens the view that the wealth, the ear ornaments and the armour, all convinced the finder that the child was well-born. Kunti did not know his fate till years later, when she was not in a position to acknowledge him as her son. The son, on his part, never forgave the mother for having abandoned him. From the minute of his birth to well after his death, this child was a constant source of dread and sorrow to the mother.

Her own father gave her away to a friend. One life-long sorrow was born of this action. Her adoptive father gave her in marriage to an impotent man; and all the rest of her sorrows were a result of this union.

Pandu, her husband, was the king of Hastinapura. Kunti, therefore, was the queen. The kind of privileges she enjoyed as queen are not known. She herself mentions just once at the very end what she had when a queen.

Pandu, as became a king, went on a conquering expedition, defeated many a king and brought immense wealth as tribute. He presented it all to his blind elder brother Dhritarashtra and went himself to live in the Himalayan forest with his two queens Kunti and Madri.

The Mahabharata says that there he incurred the wrath of a sage and was cursed that union with a woman would prove fatal to him. This whole narrative seems to be a later addition which tried to hide some congenital defect in the father of the heroes. Pandu must have known this lack in himself. There does not otherwise seem to be any reason for his retiring to a forest with his two queens in the prime of life. All the Kuru kings were addicted to hunting but that could not have been his reason, for they did not take their queens along with them to the hunts. Pandu had gone to the forest with the intention of living there. Did he intend that some other man should beget children on his queens? Did he wish to carry out this plan away from the capital so that nobody should know the identity of the fathers of the children? This appears to be the case because he did get his five sons in this manner. Why did he remain there after getting the sons? Possibly in the hope of getting some more.

Pandu begged Kunti (the senior queen) to conceive sons from some Brahman. At this request Kunti told him about the gift given to her by the sage Durvasa. This was also an opportunity for her to reveal the existence of Karna. According to the custom of those days, such a child could have become a legitimate son of Pandu, but Kunti at that time had no idea of what had happened to her son or whether he lived at all. She therefore never said anything about this child. Kunti got three sons from three gods — Yama, the law-giver and god of death, Marut, the god of winds and storms, and Indra, the king of gods. Kunti's eldest son, Yudhishthira, was born before Duryodhana, the son of Dhritarashtra. After three sons were born to Kunti, the younger queen, Madri, begged Pandu to get a magic formula for her from Kunti as she did not want the stigma of barrenness. Kunti agreed and gave a mantra to Madri.[1] Madri is supposed to have called the heavenly twins, handsomest among gods, and given birth to twin sons. When the king asked Kunti for another magic formula for his younger queen, Kunti gave a characteristic reply, 'I was a simpleton to give a mantra to this scheming woman. She was clever enough to get two sons with the use of just one. If I give her another, god knows how many sons she will have. For all I know she might establish her superiority and gain the upper hand. Now we will, neither of us, have any more children.'

This speech makes one feel that if Madri had not had twins, Pandu might have got more sons. After Kunti's refusal to have any more children, the whole family could have returned to Hastinapura. Pandu was the king and Kunti could have taken her position as the queen, and the sons would have been the heirs

1 Does this mean that permission was needed from the senior wife to allow the younger wife to practise *niyoga* (cohabit with somebody else for procreation of children)?

to the throne. This was what Kunti had striven and hoped for. But this was not to be. . . .

One day, while wandering in the forest, Pandu saw Madri unaccompanied by any children or servants. Madri was in the bloom of youth and famous for her beauty. In fact, Bhishma had paid an enormous bride-price to secure her as a wife for Pandu. Pandu could not resist the temptation and, in spite of her remonstrances, possessed her and died according to the curse in the moment of his fulfilment. Just then Madri heard Kunti coming with the children and cried out, 'Kunti, hurry and come alone. Keep the children away.' Kunti at once guessed what had happened and came rushing, wringing her hands.

'All is lost, all is lost,' she wailed. She saw the dead king lying by the side of Madri who was hastily getting up. She could not contain her jealousy. 'I protected him all these days. How could you tempt him? Indeed, you are to be congratulated that you looked upon the fulfilment in the face of the king in your arms.' Poor Madri could just murmur, 'I tried my best to dissuade him but he would not listen.' Kunti went on, unheeding, 'I am the senior wife, it is my duty to follow the dead husband. Get up, take charge of the children.'

Madri stood stunned and trembling but these words brought her out of her stupor. In one moment of horrible clarity she saw her futile life stretching before her in unending misery and chose the only way out. She said in a firm but pleading voice, 'Kunti, he died because of me. Let me follow him. Let me give him in heaven what he desired here. I could never be impartial between your children and mine. On the other hand I am sure you will look after mine as your own. Take them in your care. Allow me to follow the king.'

[Rivalry and intrigues among co-wives in Kshatriya households have been an important part of the history of India for the last three thousand years. Without Kaikeyi and Kausalya there would have been no Ramayana. Draupadi who was the foundation of the Pandavas' greatness had to acquiesce, though none too graciously, in Arjuna's bringing Subhadra as the younger co-wife. A thousand years later, Kalidasa based his political drama on the rivalry of Dharini, Iravati and Malavika. More recently, the whole course of Maratha history was shaped by the competition for power among Shivaji's wives and their sons.]

Madri burnt herself on the king's funeral pyre. Madri's lot in choosing death was indeed hard, but the life which Kunti was left to drudge alone was equally hard, if not harder.

Kunti comes out as a hard and unjust woman on this occasion. Hard she always was. She was rarely unjust. In a patriarchal, polygynous society a woman's status depended entirely on the position of the man who was either her father or husband or son. The highest that a Kshatriya woman could hope for was to be the eldest wife of a crowned king and to give birth to his eldest son. To have more sons than the co-wives was also a means of securing, if not the love of a husband, at least the position of the chief queen.

Kunti did not want the stigma of barrenness to attach to Madri, but she was certainly not going to allow the junior and more beautiful queen to have more children than herself. She knew the preference of the king for the beautiful Madri and her first outburst was due to spite and jealousy. But her claim that she had guarded the king's life so jealously was just. On the life of the king depended the security of her sons, who would have in due time succeeded their father to the throne. Pandu was the fourth man in her life to contribute to her miseries: her two fathers, the illegitimate son and now her husband. When everything had seemed within reach, his one rash act dashed Kunti's hopes. Pandu and Madri escaped, perhaps to enjoy companionship and bliss in heaven, as poor Madri had said. But Kunti had to travel the hard stony path of her life alone.

Kunti returned to Hastinapura with the five children, the two half-charred bodies and a retinue of Brahmans and servants. The citizens of Hastinapura watched the sad procession and talked among themselves.

'Are they all his children?'

'How can they be?'

'Whose else could they be?'

Kunti heard these remarks with fear in her heart but all her doubts were laid at rest by the manner in which Bhishma received her. The king and Madri were given a state cremation. The whole court went into mourning. The five children were received as princes and given into the care of the family tutors for instruction along with their cousins, the Kauravas.

These years of Kunti's life were comparatively peaceful. Hardly had Kunti heaved a sigh of relief, when fresh troubles arose. Though the Pandavas were received as princes, they were not acknowledged as the sole heirs to the throne. Dhritarashtra continued to rule though uncrowned, and quarrels broke out among the cousins. Kunti's Bhima, a hefty fellow, delighted in frightening his cousins. Apparently they in turn tried to poison him. Kunti's children proved to be quick in learning the art of weaponry. Her eldest son, Yudhishthira, was well-liked because of his good looks, learning, wisdom and deportment. People already pointed to him as the heir to the throne. It was against this background that Dhritarashtra planned to remove the Pandavas from the public eye by sending them to Varanavata. Duryodhana used this opportunity and ordered his spy, Purochana, to build a palace with combustible material to house them, in which later on he planned to burn them alive. Purochana received the princes with great pomp and took them to the palace where he too lived along with them. Though fully aware of the plot, Kunti and the Pandavas kept Purochana off his guard by pretending to lead normal lives. Kunti, as befitted the mother of the princes, kept an open house. Every day Brahmans and hundreds of poor people enjoyed their hospitality. One such was a tribal woman, who with her five sons came to the palace and slept there that night. The Pandavas took this opportunity to make their escape. In the middle of the night they set fire to the house and escaped through an already built underground tunnel.

In the narrative of this incident one sees the superiority of the critical text of the Mahabharata. It says that 'a tribal woman, as though invited by death, came to Kunti's house that day, ate, drank liquor and slept there.' Two later editions have the following versions. One says that 'the tribal woman was cruel and an accomplice of Purochana.' The other says that 'she was cruel and pretended to be friendly to Kunti.' For the sake of the plot and counterplot, the tribal woman and her sons had to die. In fact her opportune arrival must have induced the Pandavas to decide to escape on the very night that they did. This natural sequence of events was distorted by later narrators because they wanted their heroes to be above the reproach of having killed six innocent persons.

The next day, in the remains of the burnt house, the charred bodies of the tribal woman and her children were found along with another body, that of Purochana. Everyone was convinced that the Pandavas had died in the fire and that they could, therefore, spend a whole year free from harassment.

Bhima could not understand why it was necessary to walk into this fire trap at all. But Dharma had understood the situation fully. He took pains to explain to Bhima that if Purochana had suspected that they had an inkling of the Kaurvas' plot, he would have forcibly imprisoned them in the house and set it on fire. If they had run away, Duryodhana could have got them assassinated. Duryodhana had a status because of his father; the Pandavas had none. He had money, they were penniless. They therefore had to remain where they were. They had familiarized themselves with the routes of escape while pretending to hunt. By studying the stars they knew the directions, and had in the meanwhile dug the tunnel. These words of Dharma tell, more than anything else, the plight to which the Pandavas were reduced at this time of their life.

The night they escaped, Kunti had to walk for miles. After some time they reached a deep forest where even the guidance of the stars failed. They rested under a tree and sent Bhima to bring some water. When Bhima came back and saw his mother sleeping on the ground, he lamented the fact that a woman of her status had to leave the palace and sleep on the bare earth. Kunti, however, would not have judged herself to be badly-off at all. She had foiled the plot of her son's rivals. As a Kshatriya woman that was enough for her.

During this period it was she who encouraged Bhima to become the lover of, and to marry a *Rakshasa* (demon) woman. This woman was very useful to the Pandavas, and her son later on gave his life for them in the Mahabharata war. Kunti got Bhima to kill the demon Baka, and it was she who determined that Draupadi was to be the wife of all her five sons. By this move the sons of Madri and the sons of Kunti were welded into an unbreakable whole. This later proved an effective bar to all plans of Duryodhana to set them against one another. Kunti had always given to Madri's sons not only her impartial care but also her heart. Towards her own sons she was stern and dutiful, while there was a bond of genuine affection between her and Madri's sons.

On the day of the wedding, Kunti entrusted the

care of her sons to Draupadi. She felt that she could now look forward to a quiet life, but as usual, her hope was in vain. Her eldest son gambled away his kingdom. This time, being old and frail, she could not accompany her sons into exile and had to remain in Vidura's house. This position of dependence was harder for her to take than all the other privations she had suffered during her lifetime.

In this crisis she thought Pandu and Madri had been more fortunate than she. Pandu had seen the sons he had wanted, but had not lived long enough to see their downfall, and Madri in her short life had gained everything worth having. She had the love of her husband, she had the wisdom to choose the moment of her death and in doing so she had attained heaven.

Kunti's suffering and hope during the years of her sons' exile is very well described in *Udyogaparva*. Draupadi chose to go into exile with her husbands, leaving her children behind. Kunti, though not in exile, suffered greater agonies because she had to live among the enemies and witness their prowess and prosperity. When Krishna went to negotiate a treaty with the Kauravas, he called on her. The moment she saw him she fell upon his neck and burst into tears, recalling all the calamities that had befallen her since childhood.

When he left Hastinapura after the negotiations had fallen through, she sent a message with him for her sons. Her words clearly reveal her mortifications, her hopes for the future and her unbending will.

In this message she uses a phrase to describe herself which shows that in spite of her laments she had thought her own life worthwhile. She talks of herself as going from one deep pool into another.[1] She was the daughter of a king, she became the eldest wife of another king. When her son became the king of Indraprastha, she became the queen-mother. She was deprived of her right to the queenship by a rash act of her husband. She was deprived of her right to the queen-mother's position by a rash act of her son. And now this eldest son, followed by his obedient brothers, was about to propose a disastrous truce which would bring nothing but contempt from the contemporary Kshatriyas.

She sent messages with Krishna to all her sons. She admonished Bhima and Arjuna not to forget their humiliation. Her main appeal however was to Dharma. He was her eldest son, the heir to the throne. But he desired neither war nor conquest.

She said, 'Yudhishthira is the very soul of dharma. Tell him, "By your behaviour you are destroying dharma. You are aware only of one dharma, the dharma of the sluggish unlearned Brahmans who are caught in a mesh of words. But Brahmadeva created the Kshatriyas from his powerful chest so that they live by the force of their arms and protect their subjects. A king who forgets his dharma goes to hell and drags all his subjects with him. What was yours by the right of inheritance from your father has been lost. Recover it. Make it

---

1 In India, where rivers run dry in the summer, there are a few deep pools *(hrada)* which retain water all the year round. In this context, such a pool can be understood to mean a good place to be.

your own. Your behaviour pleases the enemy. No shame is greater than that I should live on other people's charity while you are still alive. Remember the dharma of the Kshatriyas. Do not throw your ancestors, younger brothers and yourself into hell."'

She further reminded her son of an old legend — the conversation between Vidura (or Vidula) and her son. The word *'vidura'* means a 'wise woman.' Her description fits both Kunti and Draupadi. She was born to success *(yashasvini),* quick to take offence *(manyumati),* born in a high family *(kulejata),* a follower of the Kshatriya dharma *(kshatra-dharmarata),* a woman of foresight *(dirghadarshini),* well known among the assembly of kings *(vishruta rajasamsatsu),* learned *(bahushruta,* literally, one who has heard much.) Her son has been described as follows: defeated at the hands of Sindhuraja, prostrate, weak-minded, joyless, ignorant of dharma, one who gave pleasure to his enemies. Vidula's castigation of her son, which takes up five chapters of *Udyogaparva,* was narrated in its entirety by Kunti for Dharma's benefit. Only a small part of it is given below:

'How can you lie prone like a corpse? Do not take defeat lying down. Show your valour even if you die in the effort. You are worthy neither of a name in this world nor of a place in heaven. I have given birth to infamy in the guise of a son. No ruling house should have a son who brays loudly like an ass but is slow to act. Live up to the name you were given — Sanjaya, the conqueror. Your wife and I should be shelter-givers to others. Today we are receiving shelter from others.'

To this the son replied, 'All the iron in the world has been collected to mould your angry, pitiless and revengeful heart. Is it the dharma of the Kshatriyas that you should talk in this manner to an only son? Do you think you can enjoy the kingdom and the riches of the earth or even your own life if I am dead and gone forever?'

The mother said, 'This is the time to goad you to action with harsh words. A love which is weak and undemanding is like the love of a female donkey. You are a Kshatriya. You must either defeat your enemies or be killed.'

The son gave a last desperate excuse. 'How can I fight, mother? How can I get soldiers together? I have no money.'

The mother had won her point. 'Well spoken,' she said, 'I have hidden wealth. I'll give it to you if you are ready to fight.'

The son fought and won back his kingdom. 'Krishna,' Kunti said, 'tell this legend to Dharma. Tell Arjuna, "It is now time to fulfil the hopes of a Kshatriya mother. Fight and crown your eldest brother as king." ' Her message to her daughter-in-law admonished her not to forget the high rank to which she was born.

Her words were like the lash of a whip. Their aim was only one — to spur her eldest son to fight. Doubtless, Kunti's heart too was made of steel.

The words in which Karna later spurned her were even harsher than these. She need not have gone to Karna. But the thought that weaning Karna away from Duryodhana would foil Duryodhana's plans effectively made her undertake this humiliating task. She told Karna who he was and asked him to join forces with his five brothers. She tried to tempt him by saying that in joining her other sons as their brother he would gain Kshatriyahood.

With bitter irony Karna said, 'Oh high-born Kshatriya lady, I believe what you say. You have committed the sin of destroying the foundation of my name and fame. Even though born a Kshatriya, I did not receive the sacrament of a Kshatriya. What enemy could do me a greater wrong? At that time you showed me no mercy, and now you challenge me to acknowledge myself a Kshatriya. The mother in you was dead then. Now you have come to me for your own selfish reasons. I have never had a brother until now. If one suddenly crops up now, what will people say to me? Whatever I have in this world I owe to the sons of Dhritarashtra. How can I leave them now?' He added further, 'I promise you this, however. You will always have five sons, whether I die, or I succeed in killing Arjuna.'

Kunti replied sadly, 'Son, all the Kauravas will be destroyed in this battle. Let it be as you say. Who can fight fate?'

These words of hers make us wonder whether she had gone to him for selfish reasons, or whether she had really wanted to save Karna from certain death.

Throughout Kunti's life we get alternate glimpses of meanness and nobility. One is repulsed by the Kunti who blamed Madri for her husband's death; but the same Kunti showered her love on Madri's orphaned children all her life. Draupadi could have been the wife of her own three sons, but Kunti did not exclude the other two. It does not appear that in doing this the unity of the five was her only motive. Once she called Madri's sons her own, they did become her own.

Her behaviour in the case of Karna was similar. It was impossible for her to care for the child born to her while still an unmarried young girl in her father's house. When she discovered him, she could not call him her own. Karna could not forget this injustice. Nor could she.

The war was over and the sad and difficult task of identifying the dead bodies and giving them the proper last rites was being performed. Kunti chose this moment to reveal to Dharma the fact that Karna was her first son and as such his elder brother.

One wonders how Kunti could undo the wrong she had done to Karna after his death. From her point of view the reason for what she did was obvious. 'You let me grow up without a Kshatriya's sacrament', was Karna's lament at their last meeting. It was Kunti's firm belief that a man could attain heaven if he was cremated according to the rites due to his status. She must have felt that it was the least she could do for Karna. During the first part of her life she had felt the need to acknowledge Karna. Just before the great war both she and Krishna had felt the necessity of getting Karna to join the Pandavas. For this a public acknowledgement of her relationship with Karna was necessary. Kunti was prepared to undergo this ordeal. But now after the war was won, such a necessity no longer existed. It was only because her sense of justice would not let her rest that she made a public confession at this time.

Whatever the others might have said, Dharma's condemnation of her was sweeping and merciless. Dharma is said to have mourned the loss of his brother bitterly. He even blamed Kunti for the entire Mahabharata war.

'Your secret has destroyed all of us — the Kurus and the Panchalas are no more. Draupadi's sons and Abhimanyu are dead. If you had told us at that time that Karna belonged to us, there would have been no war.'

He even went so far as to curse all of womankind by saying, 'Henceforth they shall be incapable of keeping a secret.'[1]

Just before the end, Kunti once again showed her unbending will. After living for fifteen years with Dharma, Dhritarashtra and Gandhari decided to spend the remainder of their lives in the forest. Dharma, Arjuna, Kunti and all her daughters-in-law showed the old couple proper respect. But Bhima could not forget the wrong done by this uncle. He, followed by Nakula and Sahadeva, took every opportunity to insult Dhritarashtra. Under the circumstances, Dhritarashtra could not complain about his nephews' behaviour. He decided to leave the palace. Vidura and Sanjaya decided to accompany him. Kunti also made up her mind to go with him. 'I have never served the older people in my

1 This incident may very well be a later interpolation.

family. Let me do so now by waiting upon my old father-in-law.'[1]

So saying she started out with them. At this the Pandavas broke out into a loud lament. Hearing the lament, Dhritarashtra said to Gandhari, 'Tell the daughter-in-law,[2] "You have suffered much. You should spend your remaining life in comfort with the children".'

Kunti would not listen to anyone. With tears in his eyes Dharma reminded her, 'You made Vasudeva tell us the story of Vidula. To honour your word, we fought the war and won our kingdom back. Where is your Kshatriya dharma now that you are leaving your sons, your daughters-in-law and the hard-won kingdom?'

Kunti could not stop her tears, but she continued walking. Then Bhima said, 'How can you go away without enjoying the kingdom your sons have won for you? If this is what you intended to do, why did you make us fight this terrible destructive war? Why did you take the trouble of bringing us and Madri's two infants from the forest into Hastinapura at all?'

The children talked on. Draupadi, weeping, followed Kunti. Kunti walked on for a while in silence. When she saw that they would not stop following her, she dried her tears and addressed Dharma, using his patronym. 'Pandava, all that you have said is true. When you lay down in despair, I had to whip you into action. You gambled away the kingdom. Happiness

---

1 One's husband's elder brother and his wife can be so addressed and the respect due to parents-in-law is given to them.

2 A younger brother's wife.

had fled from you. Your kin despised you. You were sinking and I pulled you up. I prodded you so that Pandu's house should not become infamous. I had to wake you out of your lethargy so that this daughter-in-law of mine might not be insulted again. Children, as Pandu's wife and queen, I enjoyed my kingdom fully. I performed religious sacrifices, I gave large gifts to Brahmans. I drank the sacred soma juice. I sent the message with Vasudeva not because I lacked anything. I have no longer any wish for enjoyment of this life. This is the time for me to practise austerity, serve my parents-in-law and thus attain heaven so as to meet my husband. Don't follow me. Go back.'

The Pandavas, shamed into silence, returned with Draupadi.

Kunti was leading Gandhari by the hand. Dhritarashtra had put his hand on Gandhari's shoulder. Thus in a row, they walked through the streets of Hastinapura.

In the forest, Kunti waited on them faithfully. Every day she led them to the river Ganges for their bath and brought them back. The children came once to see them. They wept again.

Vidura died first. Some time later there was a great forest fire. Sanjaya wanted to run to safety with the three older people. The old people refused to move. They bade Sanjaya to save himself.

Kunti, with her two companions, sat down in a yoga pose, calmly awaiting the fire. She died, as she had lived, unbending.

5 Father and Son?

Bhishma had made arrangements for the education and training of the sons of Dhritarashtra and Pandu. He had, however, made no special effort to protect the Pandavas. Perhaps he was unaware of the rivalry between the cousins? Maybe he was helpless to do anything about it? Or was he merely indifferent? The house threatened with extinction had survived; where there had been no heir, two were born, and from these two had come a hundred and five. Did he feel that it made no difference if some perished, as long as a Kuru occupied the throne? We cannot say, but nevertheless it is true that up to the time of Draupadi's swayamvara he was careless enough not to have noticed the ill will of the sons of Dhritarashtra towards the Pandavas, their cousins.

Vidura was the one who strove like a father for the good of the Pandavas. But Vidura's own position was so subordinate that until Dhritarashtra's cunning and Duryodhana's jealousy became known to all, he had to be very circumspect in whatever help he gave to the Pandavas. Duryodhana, Shakuni, and the others were constantly looking for an opportunity to kill the

Pandavas, especially Bhima, the strongest among them. All their plots — to drown him, to have him bitten by a snake, to poison his food — were revealed to the Pandavas by Yuyutsu, who was the son of Dhritarashtra by a concubine. The Mahabharata says that the Pandavas always behaved according to the advice of Vidura, never revealing their knowledge of this enmity or the plots against them. Vidura was not only concerned for the Pandavas, but also for their mother Kunti. Once, in their youth, when a fight seemed imminent between Karna — Kunti's illegitimate son — and Arjuna, Kunti was about to faint in fright. Vidura calmed her and skilfully intervened to prevent the fight. During the Pandavas' thirteen years of exile, it was Vidura who gave shelter to Kunti.

Vidura's partiality to the Pandavas did not remain completely unknown. When Duryodhana was plotting to send the Pandavas to a distant town to kill them, he showed he was well aware of Vidura's attitude. Summing up the position at the Kuru court, he said, 'Bhishma is completely neutral; he shows no preference either for us or for the Pandavas. Drona's son is with us, and the father will go along with the son. Kripa also will follow these two. Vidura outwardly gives no sign of it, but he really is on the side of the Pandavas. However, all by himself, he cannot do anything much against us.'

Dhritarashtra had plotted skilfully to send the Pandavas to Varanavata, and Dharma was forced to comply, even though he knew certain death awaited them all. The Pandavas bade farewell to everyone. In a speech before all, Vidura used phrases with double meaning to warn them of the likely dangers and to suggest a way of escape. After they had left, he secretly sent a trusted servant to dig a tunnel beneath the house where the Pandavas were living. When the house was set on fire, they escaped through this tunnel. Vidura's foresight had saved them.

After their marriage to Draupaḍi, Vidura openly sided with the Pandavas. The reason is obvious. His position at the court of the Kurus remained what it was. He could render help to no one. But the Pandavas were now independent, with the might of the Yadavas and the Drupadas behind them. There was no longer any need of secretly foiling the plots of their enemies. This difference is shown with great acuteness in the *Adiparva*. The Pandavas had won Draupadi. Duryodhana and his friends came home, humiliated and empty-handed. As soon as Vidura heard the news, he went to Dhritarashtra and exclaimed, 'Congratulations to the Kauravas!' The Panḍavas as well as Duryodhana and his brothers were descendants of Kuru and thus Kauravas, but the Pandavas were supposed to have perished in Varanavata, so Dhritarashtra naturally thought it was his own son who had won Draupadi. In great joy he said, 'Fine, fine, bring Draupadi in; Duryodhana, go and fetch ornaments for your bride.' Then Vidura told him what had actually happened. Vidura had had his revenge for all the harassment and plotting against the Pandavas. Dhritarashtra was clever enough to answer quickly, 'Aren't my brother's children my own, Vidura? They also are dear to me.' Vidura answered warmly, 'For those sweet words may your mouth be filled with sugar. I hope your feelings always remain so.' After Vidura went away, Duryodhana and others came to Dhritarashtra and started their old game of plotting against the Pandavas. But Dhritarashtra, realizing that secret plots would be of no avail now, called Bhishma, Drona, and Vidura. All of them advised him to be friends with the Pandavas, but Vidura's plea was made with the greatest emotion. Vidura himself then went to bring Kunti, Draupadi and the Pandavas to Hastinapura, where they were given a share of the kingdom. It was after this that Vidura became the open champion of the Pandavas.

As an individual, Vidura has a special function and position in the Mahabharata. In addition, he belonged to the *kshattas* or sutas, a class which plays a peculiar role in the story. This class had the burden of its own sorrows and so Vidura carried that as well as his own. Karna, abandoned by his unmarried mother Kunti and adopted by the suta Adhiratha, was a suta. A brother of Karna is mentioned, who was the son of Adhiratha. Karna was a suta through adoption; his brother, a suta by birth. Karna contracted marriage alliances with other suta families, giving his daughters to sutas and bringing suta brides for his sons. Sanjaya, who described the progress of the war to Dhritarashtra, was also a suta. Yuyutsu, born of a Vaishya woman and publicly acknowledged as Dhritarashtra's son, was a kshatta or suta; so was Vidura. His wife, the daughter of the king of Devaka, is called Parshavi, denoting that she was a suta. Ugrashrava, the son of Lomaharshana, and narrator of the Mahabharata story, was also a suta, as were the Kichakas, one of whom was the general of the Virata army and the brother of Sudeshna, the queen of Virata.

The sutas were charioteers, warriors, and the repositories of the lore and genealogies of the kingly families. In this last capacity, they were also story-tellers and were greatly in demand at all social gatherings.[1] The Kshatriyas had a feeling of closeness and kinship with the sutas. Within the enclosure of the palace, the sutas lived in their own houses. From the Mahabharata's description, it seems that they never lived in the palace itself. In many cases the Kshatriyas and sutas were actually half-brothers, like Dhritarashtra and Vidura, Duryodhana and Yuyutsu. Not only were the sutas near-equals of the Kshatriyas, some, like the Kichakas were actually a threat to the power of the king. Though completely dependent on the Kshatriyas for their maintenance, they could assume the role of advisers, as Vidura and Sanjaya did. Sanjaya even took an active part in Duryodhana's war councils. Beautiful suta women, like Sudeshna, could become Kshatriya queens, but the Kshatriyas never gave their daughters to the sutas. Duryodhana gave a kingdom to Karna, but never married into Karna's family. He called Karna his

---

1 The sutas are mentioned together with another class, the *Magadhas,* in the compound *sutamagadha,* but the Magadhas had a much lower status. The only duty of the Magadhas was to sing the praises of the king when he entered the court.

friend, but their relationship was never one of complete equality; to the end it was that of a patron and retainer. Such was the position of the other sutas, and of Vidura himself. Vidura and his brothers (Dhritarashtra and Pandu) were sons of the same father (Vyasa). But the mothers of the first two were Kshatriya princesses and wives of the dead king, whereas Vidura's mother was a servant of the dead king. The Mahabharata clearly says that if this had not been the case, Vidura would have become the king. Even at the end, Krishna's grandson Vajra got Indraprastha; Arjuna's grandson Parikshita got Hastinapura; Yuyutsu the suta — Dhritarashtra's own son — got nothing.

This was the whole sorrow of the sutas. Extremely near to the Kshatriyas, of the same blood as the Kshatriyas, in a position to advise them without fear, they could never become their equals. Neither they nor their offspring could sit on the throne. Because he was blind, Dhritarashtra could not sit on the throne; but Pandu, though not without defect, was made king. Vidura, physically and mentally the fittest, was left empty-handed.

Dhritarashtra loved Vidura dearly, but even that love was authoritarian. At any time of the day or night he would send a messenger to call Vidura. If he wanted to send a messenger to the Pandavas, he would always send Vidura. The Mahabharata describes how once in a fit of anger he ordered Vidura out of the palace; then he repented and called him back, seating him on his lap and begging his forgiveness. Vidura was a brother indeed, but a brother who could claim no right except that of bare maintenance. Was it this position that made him sympathetic to the cause of the Pandavas? Bhishma, the eldest of the clan, took no sides in the rivalry between the Pandavas and the Kauravas. He did make attempts to stop their quarrels, but it was Vidura who was drawn to the Pandavas. Bhishma kept warning the Kauravas that the Pandavas were mighty warriors who would bring about their destruction. Vidura also knew this, but he kept emphasizing the question of justice, not of power. Did he feel, perhaps, that he had no right to the kingdom, but the ones who did have a right should not be deprived of it?

The very meaning of vidura is 'knowing much'. Throughout the Mahabharata, we see that this knowledge was not primarily of this worldly affairs, but a knowledge of ultimate values. Time and again in his advice to Dhritarashtra, Vidura stressed the folly of greed, the need for justice, and the eternity of the soul. All this knowledge, however, was poured out before a man who neither listened to nor profited from it. Dhritarashtra had been denied the kingdom because he was blind. Still wounded at his loss, obsessed with the idea of getting for his children what he could not for himself, he had lost the ability to discriminate between right and wrong. While the Pandavas were children, he paid no attention at all to Vidura's advice. Later he would listen, but make excuses, 'What can I do? I can't control my sons. Now they are too big to listen to me.' Only once did Vidura retaliate. That was, as we have seen, after Draupadi's swayamvara, when the Pandavas brought Draupadi. At the end, when the war was over and all of Dhritarashtra's sons had died, Vidura said, 'King, what is the use of weeping now? When you were dancing with joy at the Pandavas' loss in the dice game, I had warned you, "This is no occasion for triumph and jubilation; it presages nothing but destruction." You paid no heed then. Now behave like a Kshatriya. Don't weep.' There is no gloating in these words. All Vidura meant was that what happens to a man is the fruit of his own action and must be endured with courage.

We never see Vidura bewailing his sorrows or loss. In fact, in comparison with the other characters in the Mahabharata, it might be said that his life was a happy one. He lived in his own house, spending his time in reflection, meditation, and worship. He had children; he achieved fame. But still it seems as if an indefinable sadness and melancholy filled his life.

In the Mahabharata every person — man or woman, high or low — is plunged into one activity or another. Dhritarashtra and Pandu, Gandhari and Kunti, Duryodhana and the Pandavas, Draupadi and Subhadra, Uttar and Uttara, Drupada and his children, Krishna and all the Yadavas — all these Kshatriyas lived restless, intense lives. Their lives had heights and depths, loves and hates. Whatever real peace they had, came only after death. In old age, beaten by life, they finally achieved with great effort a resignation which was not so much peace as a desperate attempt to impose calm. Dhritarashtra, Gandhari, and Kunti's last days in the forest, and the last journey of the Pandavas give no sense of peace. What was true of the Kshatriyas was true of the sutas. Sanjaya, whose task was merely to tell Dhritarashtra what was happening in the war, could not remain uninvolved. Even the Brahmans, Drona and Ashvatthama, were not spared from the tormenting activity of the mind and body.

In a sense, Vidura's calm life stands out in relief against all this. In another sense, it remains almost unnoticed. If he felt the stigma of his birth and the loss of his right to the kingdom, very early in life he must have swallowed his frustration and marked out his future path. The Mahabharata reveals the innermost thoughts of all the other characters, but is completely silent about Vidura. Was it because he was a sage, as his name suggested, or was it because he was an incarnation of Yama, the god of death, that life's restlessness did not touch him? No, we cannot say that he was indifferent to everything. He was the champion of the Pandavas. He detested cruelty and injustice. Yet he did not forget his status or duty. On the day of the battle, while the two armies faced each other, Dhritarashtra's son Yuyutsu openly joined the Pandavas. But Vidura, who had constantly argued with Dhritarashtra on behalf of the Pandavas, never left Dhritarashtra's side. When necessary, he censured Dhritarashtra, but in Dhritarashtra's sorrow he was there to comfort him.

Bhishma and Vidura sat in the same court. On some occasions, we find their speeches given one after the other. But perhaps because Bhishma belonged to the older generation, there were no conversations between them. The beginning of chapter 103, where such a conversation occurs, is clearly an interpolation. Bhishma says to Vidura, 'I have decided to bring Subala's daughter Gandhari, the Madra princess Madri, and the Yadava princess Kunti as brides to our house. What do you think of this Vidura?' Vidura answers, 'You are our father and mother. Do what you think right.' Following this exchange is a long account of each girl, ending with her marriage. This means that the eight stanzas at the beginning of the chapter are meaningless. Moreover, the question was about the marriage of Vidura's two elder brothers, and Vidura himself was unmarried. All the brothers must have been below the age of twenty, and Vidura was the youngest of the three. It is impossible that Bhishma should have asked his advice at such a time. After the marriage of his two elder nephews, Bhishma secured a bride — a daughter of King Devaka and a maidservant — for Vidura. Good childern were born of this marriage. The three or four stanzas about his marriage and children are all we know about Vidura's domestic life.

Vidura kept both himself and his family removed from the intense mental and physical conflicts described in the Mahabharata. But somehow one suspects that he had a deep hidden involvement in these events. Was there some secret buried in this outwardly serene life?

Though Vidura was the champion of the Pandavas, he was closer to Dharma than the others. When the Pandavas were going to Varanavata, Dharma was the one he warned about the dangers ahead. Every time he came from the court of the Kauravas, he would have a long talk with Dharma. The friendship of Vidura and

Dharma was not like that between Duryodhana and Karna, or Krishna and Arjuna, a friendship known to the whole world. Nor was it a friendship between equals. Dharma himself said that Vidura was like a father to the Pandavas. But beyond that there seems to have been a special intimacy between Vidura and Dharma. There is an extraordinary similarity between the two. If Vidura was famed for his knowledge of dharma and right conduct, so was Dharma known to his own generation as learned, reflective and knowing the principles of dharma. We get a measure of his wisdom in the story of the riddles of the Yaksha and again in the last journey.

Dharma was the son of Pandu, a crowned king. He had the right to the kingdom after his father's death, but complications and wrangling barred his path. As a child, he was forced to live meekly in the house of his enemies. He could not afford to forget, even for a moment, that the kingdom was rightfully his. Nor would his mother and brothers let him forget it. Gathering Brahmans and having them perform sacrifices, giving generous fees and receiving the blessings of grateful people, holding discussions on dharma, listening to the stories of old kings, playing dice now and then — these were the things he liked to do. But the role that fell to his lot demanded a man of action. Dharma could never play the part. Whatever he got was through the valour of others. His beautiful wife, his powerful father-in-law, he owed to Arjuna. For protection in both exiles, he was indebted to Bhima. Indraprastha and the incomparable Mayasabha were secured by Arjuna and Krishna. The war itself was won through the valour of his brothers and the statesmanship of Krishna. To add to Dharma's humiliation, he had to plead with Arjuna and threaten to renounce the kingdom altogether if Arjuna did not fight. And finally, when he got what he was fighting for, he had to pay so heavily that instead of his face shining with victory his mouth was filled with ashes. From the beginning to the end, Dharma's life was filled with sadness. In this respect too, his life was like Vidura's. Not getting what he fully merited was Vidura's sorrow. Having to pay an awful price for what was his by right — that was the sorrow of Dharma. Throughout the Mahabharata, Vidura's frustration is never expressed. But Dharma himself revealed his own frustration. On their last journey, when Draupadi fell down, he said she had fallen because she had loved Arjuna the most. In these words, the usually reticent Dharma bared his life-long wound. Again, in the dice game, when he wildly staked his kingdom, his brothers, and his wife, we feel that he once more revealed the pain in his heart. Did he think it a manly deed to throw to the winds all that others had won for him? Was it a gesture to show he had nothing but contempt for what he possessed?

All these things taken together suggest a question: were Vidura and Dharma father and son? There is much in the Mahabharata to support this suspicion.

The Mahabharata does not hide anybody's secrets. It even reveals that Karna is the illegitimate son of Kunti. If Dharma was born of Kunti and Vidura, then why should this fact be kept a secret? All the sons of

Kunti are alleged to have been born from gods who were invited at Pandu's wish. The children were born while Pandu was still living and were acknowledged by him as his sons. According to the legal conceptions[1] of those times, they were Pandu's sons and were thus called Pandavas. Supposing that one of the children had been born from Vidura, would he in any way have been inferior to the others? Dharma's right to the throne rested on two things: he was older than Duryodhana, and he was the son of Pandu. His rival Duryodhana was indeed younger by a few months. But he was the son of Dhritarashtra, a prince of the royal house, and Gandhari, a princess. One wonders if Dharma's claim would have been considered inferior if he were known to be the son of Vidura, a suta.

When they were planning to call gods to father the children, it is very curious that the first god Kunti called was Yamadharma, the god of death. Vidura was said to be an incarnation of Yamadharma, so we can surmise that she did not call the god, but her husband's brother, Vidura. Moreover, as the younger brother of Pandu, Vidura was, from the point of view of law and dharma, suited to father Pandu's children.[2] The child born from this union, an incarnation of Yamadharama or the god himself, was Yudhishthira, but because of the serious nature he displayed early in his life he was called Dharma. Thus, for many reasons, Dharma seems to be the son of Vidura.

---

1 *bijakshetra-nyaya*

2 Junior levirate

There are two more incidents which lend support to this contention. After Dhritarashtra and Gandhari, Kunti and Vidura had gone to live in the forest, the Pandavas would occasionally visit them. On one such visit, Dharma did not see Vidura and he asked after him. Dhritarashtra answered, 'He is practising terrible penance, he doesn't eat or drink anything. Sometimes people see him wandering in the forest.' Just then, someone came to say that Vidura had been seen naked, dust-covered, nothing but skin and bones. Dharma ran after Vidura, crying, 'Vidura, stop. I am your dear Yudhishthira.' They both continued running until Vidura stopped under a tree, deep in the forest. He leaned against the tree. Dharma once again reminded him, 'I am Yudhishthira.' Vidura fixed his unblinking eyes on Dharma, and with his yogic power he entered Dharma's body limb by limb. Vidura gave Dharma everything — his life, his organs, his brilliance. This behaviour at the time of death is like that of a father towards his son. In the Upanishads, there is a description of what a man nearing death is to do: he should lie on the bare ground, and make his son lie on top of him, saying, 'Son, I give you my organs.' The son should reply, 'I accept'. In this way the dying man transfers all his power, wealth, and intelligence to his son. This last meeting between Dharma and Vidura seems to describe the same kind of transfer. Two chapters later we are told that Vyasa came to Dhritarashtra and said, 'Vidura was Yama incarnate, born to Vichitravirya's maid-servant and me through my yogic powers; and he, in his turn, through yogic powers, gave birth to Yudhishthira, the king of the Kurus. He who is Dharma is Vidura, he who is Vidura is Pandava. And Dhritarashtra, just as your younger brother Vidura has served you, so will Yudhishthira-Dharma continue to serve you.' Thus the fact that Kunti had a son by her brother-in-law Vidura was kept a secret up to the end of the war. When at last it was revealed, it was done in such a way that it remains unclear whether the oneness of Dharma and Vidura was that of father and son, or that of their both being the incarnation of Yamadharma.

If Vidura was the father of Dharma, why wasn't he also called to father the other sons of Kunti? It is said in the later Shastras that a man should sleep with his brother's wife only when the necessity to create a son in his brother's name arises. The prevailing opinion was that this should happen only once, so it is understandable that Vidura did not approach Kunti again. One thing at least is clear: the Mahabharata, which is outspoken about all relationships, has not made a single unambiguous statement about the affection of Vidura and Dharma, or about their relationship.

As soon as we consider the possibility that these two might be father and son, the whole Mahabharata takes on a new light. If Dharma is the natural son of Vidura and the legal son of Pandu, the whole Mahabharata conflict is no longer between the sons of Dhritarashtra and Pandu, but among the sons of all three brothers. The triangular fight does not materialize because Vidura and Pandu have a common son. To prevent anyone from finding out who the fathers of his children were, Pandu went and lived far away in the Himalayas and, apparently, the natural fathers of his sons remained unknown and unacknowledged. Vidura, on his part, does not seem to have indulged in any intrigue. Even after his son was crowned, he could not become the father of the king. Vidura remained uninvolved, detached. Dharma got all that was his by right, but he got it at such cost that to the end, he, too, remained not only detached but also unfulfilled.

6 Draupadi

Draupadi and Sita are the heroines of the two great Indian poems, the Mahabharata and the Ramayana respectively. Both are daughters of the earth: Sita because she was found during the ploughing for a yajna, and Draupadi because she came out of the yajna fire itself. Both were wed in a swayamvara, and each was given to a man who proved himself the best archer of his time. One was exiled for fourteen years, the other for thirteen, and the lives of both, for one reason or another, were frustrated. But despite these similarities, the overall impact of the two is one of immense contrast, because the entire content and style of the two books are diametrically opposed.

According to English literary usage, both the Mahabharata and the Ramayana are called epics. Indian tradition, however, distinguishes between the two by calling the Mahabharata a history and the Ramayana a poem. Unlike the Ramayana, the main purpose of the Mahabharata is to record events. In doing so, it describes incidentally many things like capital cities, forests, and rivers, but these are of secondary importance and are always in the context of the main story. The scope of the Ramayana is narrower. That of the Mahabharata is wide-ranging in time, in space, and in its cast of characters. Heroes and cowards, villains and good men, impulsive fools and wise men, ugly men and fair ones are all depicted in the course of its narrative. Almost no person is portrayed as all good or all bad.

The Mahabharata is a record of human beings with human weaknesses. The entire Ramayana, on the other hand, is in praise of an ideal man. Whatever was good in the world was embodied in Rama, and it was to present this ideal to the world that Valmiki wrote the Ramayana. As Rama is the ideal man, so is Sita the ideal woman. In fact, the whole Ramayana is filled with idealized characters — the ideal brother, the ideal servant, ideal subjects, even ideal villains. It is not that the Mahabharata has no extraordinary characters. But even while depicting the extraordinary person, the poet does not let us forget the ordinary in him.

The Ramayana is principally the story of one man, with the other characters serving as a background to set the hero in relief. Beside Rama stands Sita. She has parents as well as in-laws, but her parents' home is a home in name only. Of her relations with her in-laws we hear a little more, but in this context too the characters remain sketchy. Sita goes into the forest with Rama, returns,is later cast off during pregnancy by Rama, and is finally swallowed up by the earth, but we do not hear a single protest from her father or mother. It is as if Sita were an orphan. There is a description of the greatness of her father, a ruler of the Janakas, but this greatness of his is of no help to Sita in her times of need.

Entirely different is the story of Draupadi. Her father had performed a yajna to get a child, and out of the yajna had sprung two full-grown children, a boy and a girl. The girl was Draupadi. How beloved she was in her father's house can be seen from some of her names. According to the custom in those days, a person might be known by various names. In this respect too Draupadi is different from Sita. Both had been given various names: Sita, 'the furrow'; Krishna, 'the dark one'; Janaki, 'a female child of the kingly clan of Janaka'; Draupadi, 'a female child of the kingly clan of Drupada'; Vaidehi, 'princess of Videha'; and Panchali, 'princess of Panchala'. But in addition Draupadi had two other names. We do not know the name of the particular Janaka who adopted Sita after she was found in the furrow. The name of the Drupada who adopted Draupadi after she came out of the fire was Yajnasena. From him, Draupadi has a name used often in the Mahabharata — Yajnaseni, 'the daughter of Yajnasena'. Sita's mother, the Janaka's wife, is not mentioned at all. Draupadi's mother, that is to say Yajnasena's wife, Prishati, is mentioned. Draupadi and her brother had come from the fire as grown-up children. These children were wished for and loved, not just found like Sita. Fearing that they would not feel towards her as towards a true mother, Prishati prayed to the god of fire, 'Oh, Agni, let the children forget that they have sprung from you and let them feel that they are my children.' This prayer was answered. Another name by which the boy Dhrishtadyumna is known is Parshata, and Draupadi is known as Parshati through the mother. Prishata is the name of the Drupada who was Yajnasena's father. Parshata and Parshati are thus names derived from the grandfather.

In the Mahabharata we have an account of over three generations of people bound together by the whole web of kinship. Gandhari, who on her marriage to a blind man (Dhritarashtra) had bound her eyes with a strip of cloth, had her brother Shakuni stay on at the Kuru court, intriguing on behalf of his sister's children. Kunti, the widow of Pandu, was guarding her five children with the help of her father's people. Draupadi's parents and brothers were very important allies of the five brothers: Dharma, Bhima, Arjuna, Nakula and Sahadeva. The tale of Arjuna's daughter-in-law Uttara and her brother Uttar forms a delightful sub-plot. The great grandfather Shantanu and his son Bhishma have an important role in the development of the story. Thus the background of many individual lives: brothers and step-brothers, older and younger generations, wives of brothers, uncles and nephews, relations by marriage, and many others, with their intricate rivalries and alliances, give Draupadi her many dimensions. As a background to the family relationships, we are given a glimpse of the larger rivalries and alliances in the political field of the then ruling kings, from Jarasandha of Magadha in the east to Shalva on the banks of the Indus in the west. Behind the tangled rivalries of kin are portrayed those of politics; the family and personal clashes gain a sharpness of outline against the background of the reigning houses of Yadavas, Kauravas and Drupadas. Finally, there is the war itself, a culmination of the struggle for power in the family and in the state.

In contrast to this, the Ramayana barely mentions the in-laws of the Ikshvaku (Ayodhya) house—the Janakas and Kekayas. Ravana, with whom the battle was fought, belonged to a different world, beyond the pale of the Kshatriya houses of the Gangetic valley. Like a modern love story, the whole narration is about two people; we get no glimpse of the familial and social forces which shape their mental processes and personalities.

Till the day they married Draupadi, the Pandavas travelled incognito from town to town. They had escaped the horrible death planned for them by the Kauravas, and were afraid of letting their enemies know that they were alive. In the court of Drupada they sat, under assumed identities, among a group of poor Brahmans. Arjuna's success in the contest won for the Pandavas not only a beautiful wife but also powerful allies. With these allies and the Yadavas to back them, they could ask for their share of the Hastinapura kingdom. Through their marriage to Draupadi, they got a wife, status, and a kingdom.

In the Ramayana, Rama had sat among the Brahmans in the court of Janaka. But he was not sitting incognito. It was mere chance that he happened to be with a Brahman at that time. Their marriage brought status to Sita and gave Rama a beautiful and devoted wife. From the point of view of the Ramayana, Rama needed nothing more.

As the daughter of a powerful and noble family,

Draupadi was the living symbol of the Pandavas' new position; but more than that, as the wife of all the five brothers, she was the source of their unity and solidarity. The day Arjuna won her and brought her home his mother unwittingly said, 'Whatever you have brought today, share equally with your brothers as always.' Then she saw the lovely young girl! How could she be divided among the five? Dharma told Arjuna, 'Brother, you won her; *you* marry her.' Arjuna answered, 'How can I commit the sin of marrying before you and Bhima, my elder brothers? You are the eldest; you marry her.'

Arjuna was right. From the Vedas and the Brahmanas onwards, it was considered not only contrary to good etiquette, but also sinful for the younger brother to marry before the elder. If he did so, the guilt fell not only on both the brothers, but also on the parents who had consented to the marriage. The reasons for this are clear. In ancient times, the eldest had the right of succession and inheritance. To be able to perform the *shraddha* (offerings to the dead) of his parents and the duties of a householder, he had to be married. Moreover, the younger brothers had access to an elder brother's wife, but over the younger brother's wife an elder had no right. Thus the marriage of the younger brother before the elder deprived the elder of his social, familial and religious rights, and for this reason such a marriage was considered a sin. Had Arjuna married Draupadi first, his elder brother could not have married her. On the other hand, Dharma as the elder had the right to marry her though she had been won by Arjuna. In his grandfather's generation,

Bhishma had won a girl and given her to his brother. If Dharma alone had married Draupadi, all five would have had the right to her, but the text suggests the following reason that this alternative was rejected and she was solemnly married to each. As the discussion about what to do with Draupadi went on, the eyes of the five brothers were fastened on her with unconcealed desire, which did not escape the shrewd observation of Kunti. Finally, through her wisdom and a stratagem of Vyasa the dilemma was resolved so that Draupadi became the wife of all five, and her marriage to all five thus destroyed any possible seed of dissension.

This very thing Karna later pointed out to Duryodhana. After the Pandavas had got married and come out into the open, Duryodhana was planning again to destory them. He told Karna, 'Divide Kunti's three sons from their two step-brothers, the sons of Madri; or offer Drupada money for turning the Pandavas over to us. Or if nothing else, let us at least destroy Bhima, for he is a constant thorn in my side.' Karna pointed out the futility of all such measures: 'If we couldn't destroy the Pandavas when they were friendless, we certainly cannot do so today. Now they have allies, and, what is more, they live in a different country. Besides, Drupada is a man of principle, not a greedy king. Drupada's son is devoted to Arjuna. Now that Draupadi has become the wife of the five it will never be possible to separate the brothers.' And as long as Draupadi lived, they never were separated.

Kunti had watched over the Pandavas until the day of their marriage, after which Draupadi assumed the responsibility. The five were brave, but poorly suited to the responsibilities of kingship. One was addicted to dice, another mighty but brash, the third valiant but unskilled in statecraft. The two younger sons merely copied the example of their elder brothers. Affairs of state were never handled independently by the Pandavas; they were managed by Krishna, Kunti's brother's son.

Very soon after her marriage, Draupadi saved her husbands from utter ruin. In the dice game Dharma had not only lost his entire kingdom but had also staked his own wife. Dragged into the assembly of the Kauravas, she was shamefully dishonoured. Finally, fearing that the indecency had gone too far and would have terrible consequences, Dhritarashtra intervened. To Draupadi he granted three favours. With the first she freed Dharma as the crowned king; with the second she freed the remaining four. Then saying, 'If my husbands are free and armed, that is enough for me,' she refused the third favour. Skilfully asking for the favours, without making any demand for herself, she had saved the Pandavas from degradation. Karna again summed it up: 'Up till now we have heard of many beautiful women in the world, but no woman has done anything equal to what Draupadi has done here today. The Pandavas and Kauravas were burning with anger, and in that conflagration no one can say what might have happened, but Draupadi has re-established peace. Like a boat, she has saved the Pandavas when they were about to drown in a sea of disgrace.' The taunt that they had been saved by a woman infuriated Bhima.

Though Karna had said it maliciously, it was true.

The word used for the period spent in the forest is the same in the case of Draupadi and Sita — *vanavasa* (living in the forest) — but there the comparison ends. Draupadi was driven to the forest by her husband's addiction to gambling and the consequent loss of his kingdom. Sita's forest life, on the other hand, was the result of her husband's idealism and sense of duty. Kaikeyi, the step-mother of Rama, had plotted to secure succession to the throne for her own son Bharata. She extracted a promise from her husband to send Rama into exile for fourteen years,andto give the kingdom to her own son. From this intrigue the king died of grief. Rama, as the eldest prince, could have become king immediately, but he chose, instead, to fulfil his father's promise. Rama left the capital, but Bharata refused to accept the kingdom, and returned it to Rama. Therefore, from a practical point of view, there was no reason for Rama to go at all. Rama went into exile only because he had assumed the burden of his father's promise. It was a self-imposed ordeal.

The Pandavas, however, were forced into exile. In the capital of their enemies, the Kauravas, the stakes had been announced openly before the elders. There was no alternative except to abide by their word. When they came to see the Pandavas at the beginning of their exile, Draupadi's brother and Krishna could do nothing more than express their dismay at what had happened. Going to war at that time would have meant a permanent blot on their name; and, under the circumstances,even their friends might have refused to back them. Keeping true to their word was, for the time being, the only defence against their enemies. Their behaviour, in other words, was not only moral, it was one hundred per cent expedient as well.

Just as earlier Draupadi had had the right to share in the splendour and greatness of her husbands, now she had the responsibility of sharing their suffering and disgrace. The Pandavas' other wives had taken their children and gone to their parents' homes. Draupadi sent her children to her parents — they had to be educated so it would not do to keep them in the forest — but she herself stayed with her husbands. She was not one to suffer in silence, however. She clenched her fists and cursed; she burned with anger. When her brother Dhrishtadyumna visited her in the forest, she wept continuously and cried with bitter rage, 'I have neither husbands, nor brothers, nor a father. If I had, do you think they would have stood for my being insulted like this?'

When everyone had left, she again brought up the subject, trying in vain to persuade Dharma to take revenge against the Kauravas.

Fortunately, however, Draupadi was not free to brood on the past. Even in the forest, she could not escape the responsibility of being a daughter, daughter-in-law and wife of great kings. From morning to night she was busy. She had to make preparations for the vitally important rites conducted by Dharma and the family priest. Despite the Pandavas' limited means, they could not stint on the performance of the ceremonies. Nor could they escape the obligations of hospitality — obligations prescribed by the Kshatriya code and by political considerations as well. Hundreds of guests — Brahmans and others — were continually coming and going, giving Draupadi even less solitude and leisure than she had in the palace. When she was not working, she had to sit and listen to the long-winded tales of the guest *rishis* (sages). All this time she was irreconciled to her fate and dwelt continually on her hope for revenge. Krishna with his wife Satyabhama visited the Pandavas towards the end of the exile. At parting he consoled her, 'My dear, I promise you that all these insults will be paid for.' Satyabhama embraced her and said, 'Draupadi, don't cry; you have seen the Kaurava wives laugh at you; one day you will see them weep.'

Sita's exile was unshadowed by hatred and suffering. For more than twelve years, she lived in a continual honeymoon. As the wife of the crown prince in Ayodhya, she had been surrounded by the bustle of servants, by her father-in-law and three mothers-in-law. There had been no chance to give herself completely to love. Now she was free. Her forest was like the forest in the romantic dreams of young city girls; there were deer and swans, and the delightful Godavari river with its long stretches of sandy shore. Dotting the landscape here and there were the *ashrams* (hermitages) of the rishis, offering hospitality and human companionship. Occasionally, there were just enough cruel beasts to give one a few delightful shivers. Of the burden of the real world, there was nothing — no smart of remembered insult, no yearning for absent children, no crowds of guests. The poet Valmiki has poured into the Ramayana all of his powers. Using the forest as a background, he has told the story of the gradual transformation of Sita from a young girl into a mature woman deeply in love. To Sita herself, the memory of her exile was so idyllic that during her pregnancy she craved for only one thing — to go back to the forest.

After Ravana the demon king had carried Sita off to Lanka, she faced sorrows and dangers, but they were those of a romantic, unreal world. Though she had been abducted, there was no fear of her captor raping her. She was surrounded by demonesses threatening to devour her. That the wealthy and learned Ravana should have a retinue of man-eating demons is rather peculiar. The story of Rama and Ravana with their armies of monkeys, bears and demons is more fantasy than fact.

Indeed the whole story is fantastic, romantic and other-worldly. Rama was an ideal man, Sita an ideal woman. Rama was devoted to his father, to truth, and to his wife. To show he was brave, there had to be a war. The heroine had to get into difficulties from which the hero could save her. A courageous hero, a virtuous heroine — all the stuff of the Sanskrit *kavya* (literary, especially poetry) tradition. And following the kavya tradition, category for category, there is a description of each kind of love: first love, mature love, then separation and its agonies. Even the war is but a literary device and is unreal. A great war is fought, but Ayodhya, the capital of Rama, remains untouched, waiting for Rama to return and take over the kingdom.

When the time comes, he does go back. Brothers meet brothers; sons meet mothers; daughters-in-law their mothers-in-law. The flames of war do not reach Ayodhya; they remain in the realm of romance.

Draupadi's troubles were human, brought on by people of this world and, particularly, by her own husbands. Her experiences are described realistically, unembellished by flowery language or poetic conventions. In almost every episode, insult is piled upon insult, constantly adding fuel to the hatred in her heart. Two words keep recurring in reference to Draupadi—*nathavati anathavat*, (having husbands, but like a widow). She was the wife of the five but bereft, the daughter of a rich house but like an orphan, she had brave allies but she was alone. This was the pity of her situation. Every time she was dishonoured, her husbands and fathers-in-law stood watching in silence. They had to; they were powerless. Only twice was she saved; once by a divine miracle, another time secretly by Bhima.

Furthermore, the war in the Mahabharata was a real war, bringing grief to the victor and vanquished alike. Draupadi's full-grown children were dead, her father's clan nearly destroyed. As the dying Duryodhana had said, she and Dharma would reign over a kingdom of widows. Formerly the palace at Hastinapura had been alive with a host of kin: elderly princes, and young, vigorous ones, little children, grandchildren, grandmothers, mothers-in-law and young women. When Dharma succeeded to the throne, they had all been wiped out. Since the youngest men had died unmarried, there were not even widows to burn themselves on their husband's pyres. The widowed Uttara and her son born after his father's death were the only young people left. Within the clan there was peace, but the enmities created in consolidating the kingdom had not ceased. The embittered Takshaka sat waiting for a chance to take revenge on Arjuna for the burning of the Khandava forest. For the Pandavas there was no joy in victory. Shortly after the war Krishna, who had been their support all their lives, died a tragic death and with his death his whole clan was destroyed. The end of the Mahabharata is not merely the end of Draupadi or the end of the Pandavas or of their clan. It is the end of a yuga. Each agony of that dying yuga, Draupadi suffered in her own person. When her sons were treacherously killed, she wept and complained for the last time. From then on we hear her voice no more.

There is an unfounded opinion, particularly popular after the Jain Puranas, that Draupadi was the cause of the war in the Mahabharata. One Purana has the following verse:

'In the Kritayuga Renuka was Kritya,
In the Satyayuga Sita was Kritya,
In the Dvaparayuga Draupadi was Kritya,
And in the Kaliyuga there are Krityas in every house.'

A *kritya* is a bloodthirsty, demonic female. Some misogynist has written these lines without any regard for facts. This man obviously thinks that women start a quarrel and the men fight it out; and that all the wars where much blood has been shed were due to women. In the case of Renuka, her son Parashurama went to war because King Haihaya had stolen Renuka and a cow — both the property of his father — not simply because of Renuka. In Rama's war against Ravana it is true that Sita was the one and only cause. But that Draupadi was the cause of the war in the Mahabharata — at least the main cause — is definitely not true. The seeds of war had been planted on the day Dhritarashtra was denied the throne because of his blindness and Pandu was made king.

From their earliest childhood there was enmity between the sons of Dhritarashtra and the sons of Pandu, even before the Pandavas' marriage to Draupadi. The Pandavas were more concerned with getting a share of the kingdom and in keeping peace than in revenging the insults to their wife. If the Pandavas had insisted on having their full share of the kingdom or if, to provoke the Kauravas, they had demanded even more than their due, we might have been able to say that they wanted revenge for the humiliation of Draupadi and intended to wage war no matter what happened. But in reading the speeches of Dharma and others, we can see clearly that everyting they say is directed towards avoiding war and obtaining a portion of the kingdom. Even Bhima, who is continually burning because of Draupadi's humiliation, says to Krishna, 'Tell them, "Brothers, don't destory everything; give the little bit that Dharma is asking for".' Hearing this, Krishna laughs, 'What! Is this the Bhima we've always known?' Draupadi alone keeps saying, 'Krishna, he dragged me by the hair. Have no mercy on the man who put his filthy hands on my hair.'

The Pandavas, with Krishna as their spokesman, tried to avoid war. Pitifully, like beggars, they asked only for five towns, but Duryodhana answered, 'We are not going to give you even one pinpoint of land.' Then they had to fight. As the war went on a host of old wrongs were avenged. Draupadi's wrongs were avenged only by Bhima. For the rest, there were personal rivalries, like that of Arjuna and Karna, and, most importantly, the struggle for inheritance, which from ancient times has been part of the history of the joint family in India. Draupadi did not cause the war. She wanted it, but as the true inheritors of India's patriarchal society that they were, the Pandavas were hardly men to bow to the wishes of their wives.

How little Draupadi mattered can be seen in Krishna's offer to give her and a share of the kingdom to Karna if he would join the Pandavas. Fortunately, Draupadi had no inkling of this contemptible bargain. In the opinion of some, it is true, such an arrangement would have been to Draupadi's liking; for they claim she loved Karna. However, this opinion too is entirely unwarranted. The Mahabharata makes no attempt to idealize its characters; in every character it brings out the good and the bad. If the thought of anyone other than the Pandavas ever entered Draupadi's mind, we can be sure that the Mahabharata would have mentioned it. She had never so much as looked at Karna. According to the critical edition, Karna didn't even attempt to win her in the swayamvara. In the

one point of view, even a slave has a wife, and the fact of his slavery does not destroy his authority over her. Moreover, from the most ancient times, a slave had the right to accumulate certain property that was entirely his own. The question was thus a tangled one, involving the rights of a master over a slave and a slave over his wife.

Draupadi's question was not only foolish, it was terrible. No matter what answer was given, her position was desperate. If Bhishma told her that her husband's rights over her did not cease, that even though he became a slave, she was in his power and he had the right to stake her, her slavery would have been confirmed. If Bhishma had argued that because of his slavery her husband had no more rights over her, then her plight would have been truly pitiable. Draupadi was described as 'nathavati anathavat', and if her relationship with her husband was destroyed she would have been truly widowed. From Rigvedic times there are references to abandoned wives living wretchedly in the house of their father. But there is not a single case in which a woman, of her own accord, had denied her husband. For such a woman, getting even a lowly position in her father's house would have been impossible, to say nothing of an honourable one.

Draupadi's question had put all of them in a dilemma. Bhishma hung his head. Dharma was ready to die of shame. Draupadi was standing there arguing about legal technicalities like a lady pundit when what was happening to her was so hideous that she should only have cried out for decency and pity in the name of the Kshatriya code. Had she done so perhaps things would not have gone so far. Allowing their own daughter-in-law to be dragged before a full assembly, dishonouring a bride of their own clan in the assembly of the men, was so against all human, unwritten law, that quibbling about legal distinctions at that point was the height of pretension.

Draupadi at that moment called on neither man nor god, but from the way garment after garment kept appearing to replace the ones Duhshasana tore away, it seemed as if the power of the universe itself had awakened to protect her. Still she kept insisting on the question of Dharma's right to stake her. Finally Duryodhana said, 'Ask your husband this question. We trust Dharmaraja's wisdom and judgement so much that we will abide by his decision.' Draupadi's question and Duryodhana's cunning answer cut Dharma to the quick. It was impossible to reply. But he was spared. The hall filled with ominous, threatening noises; the evil had reached its climax. Duhshasana, exhausted and ashamed, turned away. Vidura arose, greatly troubled, and said to Dhritarashtra, 'These deeds will bear terrible consequences; intervene now and save the clan.' Frightened at all that had happened, Dhritarashtra freed Draupadi and granted her three favours and with them she obtained the freedom of her husbands. Nevertheless, no one had liked her pretensions to wisdom, and Dharma never forgot it for the rest of his life. In the forest, too, Draupadi sometimes tried to show off her learning before him, but defeating Dharma in learning was impossible; each time he quickly silenced her. She had made many mistakes in her life that were forgiveable, but by putting on airs in front of the whole assembly, she had put Dharma into a dilemma and unwittingly insulted him. The fact that the insult was unintentional did not make it forgiveable. Though she was only a young bride of the house, she had spoken in the assembly of the men, something she should have known she must not do. Over and above, to pretend that she could understand questions that baffled her elders — that was inexcusable arrogance. These two things wounded Dharma and did nothing to add to her good name. In *Aranyakaparva* Dharma called her a 'lady pundit', hardly a complimentary epithet in the eyes of the Kshatriyas of the Mahabharata. Gandhari and Kunti could give advice to their sons because they were older, experienced women. For a young bride to show off her intelligence in the presence of her elders was a grave mistake. This mistake Draupadi apparently never understood and Dharma never made her aware of it. What she had done was the result of her earthy, violent, but basically simple nature.

There was, however, another mistake that Dharma revealed so openly that even Draupadi could not fail to understand it. After the death of the Yadavas — especially of Krishna — the Pandavas could no longer remain on earth. They settled their affairs and set out on the last pilgrimage. Draupadi, of course, was with them. They crossed the Ganges, then the Himalayas, and finally reached a treeless plateau. Here and there were a few rocks scattered about. Otherwise it was completely barren. Month after month the six walked in single file. Then one day Draupadi suddenly fell down. Bhima stopped. Idiotically he asked, 'Why did she fall?' After walking so far, why shouldn't she fall? Where were the six going? Did Bhima think that as usual all of them were going to reach their destination together? But the ties of life had been cut. She fell, and five, ten feet in front of her, the others fell. Dharma alone went forward with his dog.

'Look, won't you — she's fallen!' Bhima said. 'Why did she fall?'

'Bhima, keep going. She fell because she loved Arjuna the most,' Dharma answered without looking back. Draupadi fell down. Nakula, Sahadeva, Arjuna and, last of all, Bhima fell one after the other. Dharma alone went ahead with his dog.[1]

True, Draupadi had fallen, but she had not toppled over dead. A terrible fatigue had overwhelmed her. She could not take a single step more. Lying there, she heard Bhima's question and Dharma's answer. This was the Great Journey in which no one waited for anyone else. Putting her hand on her head, she lay waiting for death. But she was conscious. Dharma's words stirred memories, and in her last moments scene after scene came before her eyes. She recognised the

---

1 The discussion up to this point is based on the critical edition of the Mahabharata. What follows is my *naroti* (*naroti* = a dry coconut shell, i.e. a worthless thing. The word 'naroti' was first used in this sense by the poet Eknath.)

hurt in Dharma's words, the contempt too. For the first time in her life she pitied the king from her heart. Often in the forest she had commiserated with him about his position, but each time she took the opportunity of starting a new discussion, pointing at his wretched condition to awaken the warrior in him. So even her pity was a kind of goading. The king never gave in to her. As mildly as he could, he would try to gloss over what she said. He never told her what he was feeling. Only today, in a single sentence, he had told what he thought was her one defect, and in doing so had laid bare the life-long wound in his heart. Draupadi understood Dharma's frustration, and for a moment she felt regret. But only for a moment. Realizing his contempt, she was startled, but that too only for a moment. She smiled to herself and remembered the day of the swayamvara. After Arjuna had won her she had married all five of them, one after the other. Didn't the king realize a little of the pain she had experienced then? She had had to kill her own mind. At least in her actions she had treated all five alike. Perhaps the mind couldn't be killed completely. Actions could be made equal, but could the same amount of love be measured out of the heart for each of the five? If she had loved Arjuna most, was there anything astonishing about that?

Her mind stopped a moment. What does it mean to have loved? Ulupi, Chitrangada, Subhadra — Arjuna had loved so many women. Or had he? Had Arjuna given his heart to any woman? Women had loved him but he had given his heart to Krishna. She knew how from the beginning, from the settling of Indraprastha, Arjuna and Krishna would sit talking by the hour. In their talk, there was always some new idea — perhaps about building a city; but they talked as friends, each one speaking from his heart and listening to the other. No woman could win Arjuna's heart. Is love always like that? Is it always one-sided? I pine for someone who doesn't return my love, someone else yearns for me. Suddenly, as if shocked, she stopped. The realization pierced like lightning; there was one who had given his whole life for her. She sighed with her new understanding. Again pictures came before her eyes; Bhima along with Arjuna fighting the enemies outside the swayamvara pavilion; Bhima ready to burn his brother's dice-playing hands when she was dragged into the assembly; Bhima so angry that he had to be held down by Arjuna, Bhima comforting her when she was tired; Bhima bringing her fragrant lotuses; Bhima drinking the blood of Duhshasana; Bhima plaiting her hair with gory hands. Arjuna could have killed the Kichaka, but it was Bhima who did. How many things she remembered — greedy Bhima, rough, tempestuous Bhima, always railing at Dhritarashtra and Gandhari. In the same sense that Draupadi was earthy, so was he. She was a daughter of the earth, he was a son.

Draupadi heard a dragging sound, then a great sigh. Her whole body quivered with fear. She had been waiting quietly for the moment of her death. Was a wild animal coming? A hyena? In all the days of walking on the plateau they had seen no animals. Better that it fastened on her throat at once, without mauling her.

She closed her eyes hard. As she lay waiting for the unnamed danger to strike, suddenly a shadow fell over her eyes. A curtain had dropped between her and the sun. A low deep voice called, 'Draupadi'. It was Bhima's voice. It was he who had dragged himself, gasping with effort, over the ten, fifteen feet that separated them. On the way he had seen Arjuna, Nakula, and Sahadeva lying dead, and had thought Draupadi must be dead too. When Draupadi, frightened at his approach, had quivered, he had caught with joy this sign of life. 'What can I do for you?' The words came out with difficulty. It was the same question he had asked all his life, but in this situation it was utterly meaningless and incongruous. Draupadi smiled. Bringing Bhima's face close to hers, she said with her last breath, 'In our next birth be the eldest, Bhima; under your shelter we can all live in safety and joy.'

7 The Palace of Maya*

In the heart of the city of Pune there stand four enormous walls of what was once the palace of the Peshwas. Built by Bajirao I at the height of Peshwa power, it brought happiness neither to him nor to his descendants. However, over five generations lived there and it was the seat of Maratha power for over a hundred years. The Mahabharata tells of another building that was even more splendid, short-lived, and ill-omened. This was the Mayasabha in Indraprastha, the town which also shared the momentary splendour of the palace. Here the Pandavas paraded their wealth, but the show lasted for only a little while. They lived there hardly ten years after the palace was built. Mayasabha was born in cruelty and had its end in the frenzy of dice.

The story of Mayasabha illustrates again how large a canvas the Mahabharata presents. In the stories of Draupadi and Krishna, we have seen how the family quarrel was intimately bound up with the political rivalries of the day. The story of Mayasabha gives us a

---

* Maya was the name of the architect who built the palace, known after him as Mayasabha.

glimpse of a larger struggle in which the newly arrived Aryans and the Nagas, the older inhabitants of the land, were locked for generations. The main motive for this struggle was the possession of land. The attempts to gain land seemed to follow the usual historical pattern of marriage alliances and fighting. Many alliances between Nagas and Kshatriyas are recorded. In the Kuru genealogy itself two Naga princesses are shown as mothers of reigning monarchs. The events leading to the building of Mayasabha show what was perhaps another method of gaining land.

This is how the Mayasabha came to be built. After their marriage to Draupadi, the Pandavas were in a position of power. The plan to kill them had failed and they had reappeared flanked with strong allies. Dhritarashtra was forced to give them a share of the kingdom. Keeping Hastinapura, the hereditary capital, for himself and his sons, he gave Khandavaprastha to the Pandavas. Khandavaprastha was a little-known town on the border of the kingdom, surrounded by great forests and not far from the banks of the river Yamuna. After going to Khandavaprastha, Yudhishthira began the task of transforming the small town into a capital city. He brought artisans, rich merchants and tradesmen, and settled them in the town. In spite of all his efforts, however, the new capital was smaller and less grand than the capital at Hastinapura.

Khandavaprastha means 'a town near the Khandava forest'. The same town is also called by the grandiloquent name, Indraprastha, 'the city of the gods'. Did the Pandavas give it this name to say that their capital was more splendid than Hastinapura? The Mahabharata says so explicity.

Shortly after their arrival in Indraprastha, Arjuna had to go into exile for a year. Towards the end of this exile he went to Dvaraka, where he married Subhadra. Arjuna then returned to Indraprastha. Soon after, the Yadavas came with his bride, carrying rich gifts for the Pandavas. The Yadavas stayed in the capital for many days of festivities. It was a hot summer. Arjuna took it into his mind that they should go for a day's outing to the forest near the city. They took Dharma's permission for the plan. But neither Dharma nor Bhima nor any of the older people were included. Apparently, only the younger people went. In the party were Krishna, Arjuna, their wives and servants. They ate, they drank, they sang and danced. All the time the shade of the great trees protected them from the sun. Krishna and Arjuna sat a little apart from the others, discussing all possible subjects, telling each other of their conquests in war and love. While they were seated there, a Brahman approached them and said, 'I am hungry. I have a great appetite which has no bounds. Satisfy my hunger.' When they started to offer him food he appeared in his true form as Agni, the god of fire, and said, 'Give me the Khandava forest as food. Let me burn it. Every time I start to burn it Indra sends rain and defeats my purpose.' Krishna and Arjuna consented to help him provided that Agni supplied them with superb chariots and weapons. To Arjuna he gave a divine chariot, white horses with the speed of wind, and the great bow Gandiva. To Krishna he gave the discus and other weapons. Then Agni started devouring the forest. As it burned, Krishna and Arjuna guarded all sides so tightly that the creatures fleeing from the blaze found not a single chink to escape through. Furiously driving their chariots, the two slaughtered everything in sight. The creatures driven back into the forest were burned alive. Those who ran out fell under their weapons. Indra came with a host of gods to save the forest, but was quickly routed by the two heroes. Enraged, Indra wanted to fight further, but the gods pointed out that his friend Takshaka, a resident of the forest, was safe because he had gone away, and urged Indra to retire. The forest continued to burn for a week. All this time Krishna and Arjuna constantly circled it, butchering the escaping creatures. Finally, having consumed the flesh and fat of every last creature in the forest, Agni went away satisfied.

From this holocaust only seven creatures (were they humans?) escaped. Takshaka's son was saved by his mother's quick wit and courage, but the mother herself died in the effort. Maya an *asura* (demon), living in the house of Takshaka, was spared when he came running out of the forest crying, 'Arjuna, save me'. The four children born of a Brahmān and Sharngi, a bird-woman, were also shown mercy. The other Nagas of Takshaka's house were killed along with the birds and animals. In gratitude for having been saved, the asura, Maya, built a great palace at Indraprastha for the Pandavas. For the building of the palace — Mayasabha — he brought artisans and materials from many lands.

After Mayasabha was completed, the Pandavas

decided, on Krishna's advice, to set out on a conquest of the four quarters of the world. This task was accomplished by the four brothers of Dharmaraja. Dharma was thus in a position to perform the great *Rajasuya yajna,* the celebration of a world-conqueror. Allies, relatives and conquered kings were invited to attend the sacrifice and enjoy the hospitality of the Pandavas. A special invitation was sent to the relatives at Hastinapura. The yajna was a lavish exhibition of the might, splendour and munificence of the Pandavas. The cousins from Hastinapura were dazzled, and burned with envy. Mayasabha was built very cunningly. Birds, animals, and trees were made of precious stones so artfully that they seemed real. Flowing water was made to look like dry land, and dry land almost rippled like water. What seemed like doors were solid walls, while what was apparently a solid wall would turn out to be a door. Poor Duryodhana was thoroughly confused. He bumped his head against the walls, tucked up his garments only to find that he was walking on dry land. Finally, stepping on to what he thought was solid ground, he fell into a pool. Dharma helped him out of the water and ordered the servants to give him dry clothing. But Draupadi and Bhima laughed loudly and derisively at Duryodhana's discomfiture. The Pandavas had not only flaunted their new splendour, but they had also deliberately insulted Duryodhana. Duryodhana was not likely to forget this humiliation in a hurry.

Soon afterwards, the Pandavas lost everything in gambling and had to go to the forest for thirteen years.

After coming back and winning the war, they went to live in their hereditary capital at Hastinapura. They did not return to Indraprastha. The only mention made of Indraprastha is at the very end, when the city is given to Vajra, the grandson of Krishna. The fabulous Mayasabha is never mentioned again.

Thus Mayasabha came out of the burning of the Khandava forest. Why were all its birds, animals, and Nagas destroyed? How could Arjuna, who prided himself on his name Bibhatsu — 'one who does not do anything repulsive'— indulge in this cruel hunt? When they had merely gone for an outing on the Yamuna, what made them think of burning the forest? The Mahabharata says that Agni himself had appeared in the form of a Brahman and made the demand. Granting that they could not refuse a Brahman, can we explain the ruthless way in which they carried out their task? Not only did they burn the timber, but they also drove back into the forest all the creatures they could and killed the rest. Only a few were allowed to escape.

There are two possible explanations of the burning of the forest: either the fire was a natural catastrophe and somehow Krishna and Arjuna were credited with it, or the two did actually and deliberately burn the forest. Even if the first were true, it is obvious that burning a forest was considered a brave and praiseworthy feat. But there is no reason to question the Mahabharata's account that they did do it themselves, with great effort and persistence, perhaps having to rekindle the fire because of rain. Then why did they do it?

The pastoral Aryan people kept large herds of cattle and practised agriculture with the help of animal-drawn ploughs. Their history records many instances of either burning or cutting down forests. All the way across India, stretched thick forests which have been described in the Vedas and the Mahabharata. Several famous forests have also been described in Buddhist literature. Not only that, even historical inscripitions mention great forests. The kingdoms mentioned in the Mahabharata were all small. In the area of present-day Punjab and Delhi there were five: Kuru, North and South Panchala, Trigarta and Virata. Their boundaries did not touch. Each kingdom was but a small capital surrounded by a few score villages with their fields. Beyond were the forests. The part of the forest nearest to the villages was used by the king for hunting and for grazing his cattle. Some of the big forests had names: Kamyaka, Dvarta, Khandava, etc. These were all western forests. Later, the eastern forests, apparently smaller than the above — like Velu and Jeta—were associated with Buddha. Now the forests have vanished, and from the Indus to the Bay of Bengal the land is one vast ploughed field.

Khandava was a great forest on the banks of the Yamuna and its small tributary, the Ikshumati. The name 'Khandava' means 'made of rock candy'. Ikshumati means 'full of sugar cane'. The Madhu forest, which was also supposed to be on the banks of the Yamuna and is described in a later Purana, also means 'a sweet forest' or 'a honeyed forest'. From all these names it is clear that the forests contained something sweet. Was it *madhu* (honey)? Was it *ikshu* (cane)? Was it something else? Today the central Indian forests contain a large beautiful tree called *mahuva*. This tree, called *madhuka* in Sanskrit, is a source of bounty for the tribal people. From its leaves they make plates; from its fragrant honey-filled flowers they make wine. The dried blossoms are eaten as a delicacy, and from the sticky juice of the flowers all kinds of sweetmeats are made. Perhaps it was because it was filled with such trees that the Khandava forest was called 'sweet'. The sweetness of the forest, however, could be valued only by the people living in it, and not by the Aryans.

Like the other kingdoms, the Pandavas' kingdom was a capital surrounded by villages and fields, but it was comparatively small and the brothers were trying to expand it. Dharmaraja was making the small town into a great capital. Perhaps Krishna and Arjuna burned the forest to provide more land for cultivation. This was the duty of a ruling king. In this way he could expand his realm without encroaching upon other Kshatriyas—something forbidden by the Kshatriya code.

Krishna and Arjuna were great warriors. They had fought and won many battles. But in none of these battles did they gain any land by conquest. The Kshatriya life as presented in the Mahabharata had a certain definite pattern. Each known house had its small territory which passed from father to son. Wars were fought, tribute was demanded, but no Kshatriya house was deprived of its kingdom. An enemy was spared if he asked for mercy. If he fought and was killed, his son was put on the throne. A Kshatriya never killed women and children. Nor was he supposed to put to the sword any defenceless person. His most sacred duty was to defend the helpless. The charge that he had not done so was the worst that could be made against him.

The need for expansion explains the burning of the forest, but the question still remains: why was it burned so mercilessly? There is a very curious contradiction in the narration. When Agni first appeared, he said he wanted to burn the forest. No specific mention is made of his wanting to feed on the creatures in it. But when we come to the end of the narration, we are told that Agni went away satisfied with all the flesh and fat he had devoured.

Moreover, this forest was not merely a forest with birds and animals in it. We are told that Takshaka, the king of the Nagas, lived there. But who were the Nagas? The word *naga* is generally used for serpents.[1] However, in the Mahabharata, the Nagas seem to be human beings. The Mahabharata also mentions a bird woman, who had children from a Brahman, living in the same forest. The bird might be the clan name of certain people living there. In the same way, many of the animals may not have been animals at all but people belonging to clans having animal names.[2] But only regarding the Nagas is the word *raja* (king) used. Apparently the Nagas represented the ruling class. The Mahabharata

---

1 The word is also sometimes used for elephants.

2 The Mahabharata has many stories of children born to Brahmans through 'animal' females.

has given the names of the various Naga rajas belonging to different regions.

From the western Himalayas up to the middle reaches of the Ganga and to the south of the Narmada, the country was shared by the Aryans and the Nagas. The Nagas apparently lived along the rivers in the forests, while the Aryans preferred a more open country. The house of the Nagaraja, Airavata, was on the banks of the river Iravati. The house of Takshaka was apparently in the Khandava forest on the banks of the Yamuna. Many an Aryan king must have acquired new lands by burning or cutting parts of a virgin forest not owned by anyone. However, in the Khandava fire it appears that Krishna and Arjuna had a more audacious plan to possess an entire forest in a part of which happened to be the kingdom of the Takshakas.

This plan, it seems, did not go counter to the Kshatriya code. The code applied only to the Aryan Kshatriyas and not to outsiders. At least a part of the forest was Takshaka's domain and obviously the Pandavas wanted to possess it to distribute it to their own subjects. The land was usurped after a massacre, a massacre which is praised as a valorous deed. This was because the victims were not Kshatriyas or their Aryan subjects. All the high-sounding morality of the Kshatriya code was limited to their own group. Here again Krishna and Arjuna played the familiar role of the conquering settler. The Spaniards and Portuguese in South America, English in North America and Australia are but later historical examples of the same process. Did Krishna and Arjuna feel that they had to kill every creature in order to establish unchallenged ownership over the land?

The Mahabharata narration is very curious in that the human qualities of the Nagas are played down, and the other inhabitants of the forest are described purely as birds and animals. The whole story sounds like a week-long hunt of animals. Even granting that there were only animals, this type of killing still went contrary to the Kshatriya code. There were explicit rules of hunting. Mating animals, females carrying their young, and very young animals could not be killed. Pandu was supposed to have been cursed with impotence because while hunting he had killed a mating animal. The Ramayana opens with the curse of Valmiki on a hunter who had killed one of a pair of mating birds. Nor could the animals be killed in such measure that they would become extinct. We can see this clearly in the following story: During their exile, the Pandavas were living in a forest. To feed their retinue they hunted and killed many animals every day. One night, a stag appeared to Dharmaraja in a dream and said, 'King, you are killing so many of us that we are on the way to extinction. Go into some other forest; give us respite. When we have multiplied enough, you may come back.' The next day Dharmaraja went to another forest with his brother.

There were rules which applied to all animals, but apparently no rules which applied to all human beings. If you spared an animal today, you could always kill it tomorrow. But if you spared a human being — even to make a slave out of him — he would in the course of time acquire certain rights. There was indeed great danger in sparing the lives of those who owned the land. Krishna and Arjuna, therefore, must have felt the necessity of completely wiping out the enemy.

The people who were killed in the Khandava forest belonged to the clan of Takshaka Naga. Not all the Takshakas, however, were eliminated. Nor could they forget the wrong done to them by the Pandavas. Takshaka himself is said to have taken the shape of an arrow or ridden on the tip of an arrow in order to kill Arjuna. He was cleverly foiled in the attempt by Krishna. Either the same Takshaka or his son succeeded in killing Parikshita, Arjuna's grandson, who ruled Hastinapura after the Pandavas. Janamejaya, the son of Parikshita, in turn massacred half the Nagas. The Mahabharata starts with this Janamejaya who is told the story of his forefathers. We thus see that the main Mahabharata plot has woven into it a subsidiary theme — the feud between the Pandavas and the Takshakas — which incidentally tells us of the colonization of the land by the Aryans. Apparently, during this period, the country around the river Yamuna was made free of Nagas. This conjecture is supported by an incident of Krishna's life described in the *Harivamsha*. Krishna is supposed to have subdued a Naga chieftain in a particular area of the Yamuna. In return for his life the chieftain promised that he would leave the area.

The burning of Khandava starts with the request of Agni who had come in the form of a Brahman. It is implied that being Kshatriyas, Krishna and Arjuna could not refuse. Even this excuse is flimsy. Not every request of a Brahman was fulfilled by the Kshatriyas. The Brahman Parashurama had ordered Bhishma to marry Amba; Bhishma had refused. In the burning of Khandava no rules of conduct seem to have been observed. The sole aim was the acquisition of land and the liquidation of the Nagas. But the cruel objective was defeated. Just as Hitler found it impossible to wipe out a whole people, so did the Pandavas. All that they gained through this cruelty were the curses of hundreds of victims, and three generations of enmity.

The only man deliberately spared was Maya, the asura. In gratitude he built the famous palace. No other Kshatriya had a palace comparable to this. The Aryans built their palaces of wood, but there were people before the Aryans who knew how to build with brick. These builders were the asuras. They knew how to make ceramic tiles of different colours. Maya must have used bluish-green tiles to create the illusion of water and lined shallow pools with reddish-brown tiles to create the illusion of land. Many visitors must have been confounded by the builder's tricks. But the Mahabharata records only the humiliation of Duryodhana and the loud laughter of Draupadi and Bhima. Duryodhana was already burning with jealousy at the splendour of the Pandavas. It is no wonder that their derisive laughter cut him to the quick. Dharma's very act of helping him up from the water and ordering dry clothes seemed to be a part of the plot to humiliate him. Duryodhana was so incensed and insulted that he declared that if he could not bring down the Pandava's pride he would rather die. He was quieted only when his mother's brother Shakuni hatched the plot of inviting Dharma for a game of dice. The Pandavas lost everything they possessed, and went into exile with nothing but their weapons and the clothes on their backs. For hardly ten years had they enjoyed the fabulous palace they had obtained by burning a great forest and butchering its inhabitants.

We do not hear that Indraprastha or Mayashabha had fallen into ruin during the thirteen years of the Pandavas' exile. But when the Pandavas came back and defeated their cousins they occupied the capital of Hastinapura. They did not go back to Indraprastha. How long Vajra ruled Indraprastha we do not know. Neither do we know if Vajra's successors ruled there. New people were coming into India, in wave after wave. The Kshatriyas, weakened after the Mahabharata battle, apparently could not fight the invaders. The Puranic record says that soon after Janamejaya, the Kurus had to leave Hastinapura and found a new capital further south of Kosambi. None of the kingdoms mentioned in the Mahabharata are heard of again. Both Indraprastha and Hastinapura vanished. Hastinapura, however, left a long tradition behind it. The Kurus had ruled there for centuries. Its name is associated with the hundreds of legends about its kings. In the Mahabharata, we have descriptions of the roads of Hastinapura, we are told what the citizens talked about. The house of Vidura, Kunti's protector, was there; Dhritarashtra's court was there, and so was the apartment from which Draupadi was dragged. The Kaurava women whose lament is recorded at the end of the Mahabharata lived there.

No great ruling house is associated with Indraprastha. Except for the burning of Khandava, no other story in Sanskrit literature is set in it. Indraprastha had no substance; it never took a definite form. Mayasabha was not only ill-omened; it was even more insubstantial than the city in which it was built. Born in violence, its dazzling demonic splendour turned out to be a fleeting dream.

8 Paradharmo Bhayavahah

Taking over another's dharma is dangerous.

Bhagavadgita, XVIII

In the Mahabharata, the role of the Brahmans though not central, is certainly a vital one, even when we can dismiss some of the Brahman figures and their stories as entirely extraneous. Parashurama and all the references to him fall into this category. This man fought a week-long battle with Bhishma and was defeated. Also he trained Karna in weaponry, and then cursed him that he would forget his knowledge in the time of need. Parashurama was supposed to have lived before even the incarnation of Rama. After finishing the terrible task of annihilating the Kshatriyas, he retired to do severe penance. In the Rama story, he is brought back once to show the greatness of Prince Rama, though he has nothing to do with the plot of the Ramayana. Similarly, Parashurama has been thrust into the Mahabharata in order to demonstrate the moral and physical superiority of Bhishma, the Kshatriya, over this Brahman. In the second instance, his interference was in order to save Karna's face. Karna was reputed to be a great hero, but he was defeated and killed by Arjuna. Parashurama was brought into the story to give an excuse for this defeat. In this story, too, the Kshatriya hero came out better than Parashurama. Without complaint Karna accepted the curse, as he had accepted the training of his teacher. This story does not deserve much attention. At the time of the cattle raid on the Viratas, Arjuna had completely routed Karna in an open battle. It was, therefore, hardly extraordinary that he should have defeated him again in the last fight. The object of the story is obviously to show that Karna was a great warrior and he would not have been defeated except for the curse of Parashurama. According to legend, each of the four disciples of Vyasa has given a slightly different version of the Mahabharata story. The present version is supposed to have been told by Vaishampayana. The same story is also said to have been told by Jaimini. The Kauravas and the Pandavas quarrelled, they fought a war, the Pandavas won, and their descendants ruled Hastinapura —these were facts that Jaimini could not deny. But his version of the story is said to be partial to the Kauravas. Of this version only the *Ashvamedha* chapter is extant. In it he shows that Arjuna was defeated many times, and each time had to be rescued by Krishna and others. The fact that Karna was killed by Arjuna was indisputable. The story of the curse is obviously an invention to avoid the conclusion that Arjuna was the greater hero. In this whole episode there is nothing that contributes to the main story of the Mahabharata.

Into the story of Takshaka's curse, too, is woven a

long, monotonous narrative about Brahmans. Parikshita, when out hunting, came across a Brahman in deep penance. As a joke, he hung a dead snake around the Brahman's neck. A little later, the Brahman's son came there and got very angry at this practical joke. He cursed the king that in a few weeks' time he would die of snake bite. When the Brahman woke from his deep meditation, the son told him what had happened. The Brahman scolded him for thus giving in to anger, and, as he knew an antidote to snakebite, he hurried to Hastinapura to save the king. On the way, Takshaka met him and cunningly turned him back, thus preventing him from saving Parikshita. Actually Arjuna, the grandfather of Parikshita, had, without provocation, burned the Khandava forest and massacred the Takshakas, a Naga clan. A Takshaka later killed Parikshita. Janamejaya, the son of Parikshita, in turn, wrought great destruction among the Nagas. It is a straightforward story of a three-generation feud. The lengthy rigmarole about Brahmans seems to be a later interpolation.

The late Professor V. S. Sukthankar has pointed out that the Mahabharata saga came into the hands of the Bhrigus, a Brahman clan. These Brahmans inserted the stories of their own family into the narration of the Mahabharata. All the Brahman stories referred to above are part of these later interpolations. They have no relationship whatsoever with the original story of the Mahabharata. We can, therefore, dismiss them. If all these accretions are dropped, the Mahabharata gains in beauty, economy, and movement.

Even the great sage Vyasa, who wrote or told the Mahabharata and who is the ancestor of the Pandavas and Kauravas, has no important part to play in the story. He makes an occasional appearance: tells the Pandavas to go to Panchala, gives advice to Duryodhana, quiets the angry Gandhari. He censures Ashvatthama, and he consoles Arjuna after the destruction of the Yadavas. But after begetting children upon the queens of the dead Vichitravirya, his role has little importance in the Mahabharata.

The two Brahmans who have an important role in the story and are an integral part of it are the father and son, Drona and Ashvatthama. Drona enters the Mahabharata when the Pandavas and Kauravas are young boys. This Brahman, skilled in the use of all weapons, was the brother-in-law of Kripa, the hereditary teacher of the Kuru clan at Hastinapura. Unable to find a good position at any court, he had been driven to desperation by poverty. In addition, he was smarting from an insult he had suffered at King Drupada's hands. In his need he had gone to King Drupada and appealed to him in the name of their friendship of student days. Drupada had laughed derisively at the word friendship and had said that friendship could not exist between people of such unequal status. Drupada might have given him a post at his court as a deserving Brahman, but he could not tolerate Drona's claim to equality on the basis of their companionship of student days. Wounded at this slight, Drona left the court of Drupada and went to Kripa. Bhishma appointed him as a teacher of weapons to the young princes. After their training was over, Drona demanded as a last token of respect that his pupils defeat King Drupada. Arjuna did so, and brought Drupada prisoner before Drona. Drona spared the life of the king in return for half his kingdom, saying, 'King, we are equals now'. To deprive a defeated king of his kingdom was against the Kshatriya code. It was especially improper for a Brahman to do so. Drona had had Drupada defeated and brought before him as a prisoner. If he had just reminded the king of his insult and let him go, he would have achieved his revenge, and would have demonstrated the Brahman virtues of forgiveness and greatness of mind. Instead of that Drona kept North Panchala, with Ahichhatra as the capital, for himself. Drupada remained the king of South Panchala. In spite of his having usurped North Panchala, Drona seems to have remained at the court of the Kurus.

Whatever Bhishma said was seconded by Drona. But the earnestness with which Bhishma tried to settle the quarrels and save the clan is not evident in Drona's behaviour. This attitude became especially clear during the last days of the war when he fought heart and soul on the side of the Kauravas.

Ashvatthama was the son of Drona. Like his father, instead of learning the Brahmanical lore, he became an expert in the use of arms. Arjuna always suspected that Drona kept the knowledge of certain magical weapons from him, and was teaching their use to Ashvatthama. Perhaps because of this, there was a covert rivalry between Ashvatthama and Arjuna. Drona tried to reassure Arjuna that he had taught him everything he knew. We do not know if Arjuna was satisfied. We only know that both father and son fought against the Pandavas.

The chief reason for Arjuna's reluctance to do battle was his unwillingness to fight Bhishma and Drona. At the time of the war, Bhishma's age must have been between ninety and a hundred. Drona was a contemporary of Drupada, and thus must have been as old as Arjuna's own father would have been. Arjuna was thirty-five, and Drona must have been at least twenty years older — that is fifty-five or sixty. The Mahabharata says he was eighty-five. At the time of the cattle raid on the Viratas, Arjuna had trounced both Bhishma and Drona. In a war, Arjuna could have again easily defeated both of them, but they were inviolate, one because he was his grandfather, the other because he was his teacher.

Bhishma had fought a mock battle for ten days in a last effort to dissuade both sides from pursuing the war. The three days of Drona's generalship, however, were days of fierce fighting. The way in which Drona got the generalship is worth noting. At the news of Bhishma's fall the army was in disarray, and shouts of 'We want Karna, we want Karna' were heard from all sides. Karna, set aside for so many days, came riding up in his chariot in great style. While reading this description, one doesn't have the slightest doubt that now Karna is going to become the general. But suddenly everything changes. Karna of his own accord advises Duryodhana, 'It is best to choose a general acceptable to all, one whose choice will not offend anybody. Make

Drona the general.' Duryodhana complies. The reason Karna gives for choosing Drona is significant. Clearly, some people must have been opposed to Karna's becoming the general. From the very beginning of the war, the question of the generalship had plagued Duryodhana. Apparently, the Pandavas were never troubled by considerations of who was young, who was old, who was a Kshatriya, who was not a Kshatriya. From the first day to the last, Dhrishtadyumna was the general of the Pandavas. Duryodhana, on the other hand, had to waste the first ten days under the generalship of Bhishma. Then, instead of Karna, he had to make Drona the head of the army. After the death of Drona, Karna was at last made general, but it seems that his appointment hurt Shalya. Duryodhana had the geater army, but he was harassed by conflicting claims for precedence from his Kshatriya allies and his own kinsmen. Drona was apparently a compromise choice.

While Bhishma was living and active Drona had enthusiastically echoed whatever he said. But after Bhishma's fall quite a different Drona appeared. Bhishma had been his employer. Duryodhana was both his pupil and employer. Drona felt it was now his duty to show his loyalty to his new master. Moreover, as we have seen, he was a compromise choice for the generalship, and must have felt anxious to prove he was worthy of the position. He told Duryodhana, 'You keep Arjuna away, and I will wipe out the rest of the Pandavas.' Though he was unable to destroy the Pandavas, he did fight vehemently. The three days of his generalship were days of great slaughter. Important people on both sides died. Chief among these were Arjuna's son, Abhimanyu, and Dhritarashtra's son-in-law, Jayadratha. Perhaps because of the tactics to divert Arjuna from the main battle, Drona and Arjuna never came face to face. Because of the absence of Arjuna it was possible for Drona to kill Abhimanyu. Drona showed no mercy in killing him. One cannot help thinking that Bhishma would not have killed Arjuna's son — his own great-grandson — so ruthlessly.

The account of Drona's death is very interesting. Bhima killed an elephant named Ashvatthama, and everywhere the rumour spread that Ashvatthama had been killed. Thinking that the rumour must be false, Drona went to ask Dharma about it. Dharma muttered to himself, 'Who knows, maybe a man, maybe an elephant.' Drona did not hear Dharma clearly, and concluded that his son had been killed. However, instead of sitting stunned as the Pandavas had hoped, Drona continued fighting savagely. Dhrishtadyumna rushed fiercely on Drona but received a terrible wound from Drona's arrow. Bhima came running to help Dhrishtadyumna. He tightly held on to Drona's chariot and shouted, 'We Kshatriyas would have a chance to survive if you Brahmans minded your own profession and did not take up arms. Non-violence to all creatures is the duty of the Brahmans, and you are supposed to be a great Brahman. For the sake of your own son, you have killed many men of the warrior tribe of Mlechh. They were following their own dharma. But you abandoned yours and butchered them. Have you no shame? The son you did all this for is already dead.

Don't you believe what Dharma told you?' At these words Drona's spirit sank. In this short respite Dhrishtadyumna regained his strength. Bringing his chariot alongside Drona's, he leaped into the Brahman's chariot. From the Pandavas' side Arjuna saw what was happening and cried, 'Stop, Dhristadyumna, don't kill our teacher. Bring his chariot here.' While Arjuna was still speaking, Dhristadyumna took his sword and cut off Drona's head. Even if Dhrishtadyumna had not killed him at that instant, there was no question that Drona was trapped and could have been driven to the Pandavas' side. Drona died in helplessness and anger, shouting, 'Karna, Kripa, Duryodhana, fight on, I am gone.' Even his last outburst was not that of a resigned, dispirited man.

Drupada had lost half his hereditary kingdom to an enemy who had not even fought him, but had defeated him through a third party. After his defeat, Drupada had performed a sacrifice to ask for a son who would take revenge. Dhrishtadyumna, the child born from that sacrifice, had fulfilled his mission.

Forgiveness, serenity, self-control — none of the Brahman virtues described in the Gita seem to apply to Drona. Drona, however, is nowhere depicted as altogether contemptible. He was at the most being true to the master whose bread he had eaten. The same cannot be said of his son. Ashvatthama had completely discarded all the qualities of Brahmanhood. Not only that, he was utterly debased. Caught in an endless chain of injury and retaliation, his deeds were unequalled in horror and cruelty. Ashvatthama entered the Kuru court as the son of a desperately poor Brahman. After his father was established at the court, he along with the younger princes learned the art of using weapons from Drona. In the use of *astras* (magical weapons) Ashvatthama was supposed to be the equal of Arjuna. However, not satisfied with what Arjuna had learned from one guru, Dharma had sent him elsewhere to learn how to use more weapons. Ashvatthama apparently never did that. In the eyes of the younger generation, Arjuna was the ideal warrior, a reputation Ashvatthama never had. In the court of the Kauravas his behaviour was arrogant. While his father sided with Bhishma, he championed Duryodhana. But Duryodhana never counted him as a warrior. Nobody ever suggested Ashvatthama's name for the generalship; indeed, there was no chance that anyone would ever have thought of him.

After the death of Shalya and Shakuni, the Pandavas began wiping out the rest of the Kaurava army. Seeing that it would be impossible to gather his fleeing soldiers, Duryodhana also slipped away. While escaping, he sent Sanjaya with a message to his father, 'I am hiding in a pool. All have been killed. I am the only survivor.' He reached the hiding place and, exhausted and sad, lay in a stone shelter within the pool. On the way to Hastinapura, Sanjaya met Kripa, Kritavarma and Ashvatthama. They too had fled from the battlefield. They asked for news of Duryodhana, and Sanjaya told them everything.

Ignoring the rest of the fleeing Kaurava army, the Pandavas and Panchalas were bent on finding

Duryodhana and killing him. Though they searched everywhere they could not find him. They returned disappointed. If they didn't find him today, they must tomorrow. Until Duryodhana was killed, they were convinced, they could not say the war was over.

While the Pandavas' chariots searched everywhere, Ashvatthama and his two companions stayed hidden. After the Pandavas returned to their camp and everything was quiet, the three came out and went to the pool where Duryodhana was hiding. Ashvatthama called to Duryodhana. A conversation ensued, with the three standing on the bank and Duryodhana sitting inside the pool. While the other two merely listened in silence, Ashvatthama kept insisting, 'Come out and fight the Pandavas.' Duryodhana was unwilling to fight. Ashvatthama on his part kept saying, 'Now that so many have died on both sides, it will be easy to fight. We are with you.' Perhaps to avoid further argument, Duryodhana said, 'Let me rest for a day. Tomorrow we can decide what to do.'

This last day of the war is very important. Duryodhana's actions show that he was mainly trying to save his life. He was hiding in a pool in a distant wood, and had sent a message to his father informing him of what had happened. His whole army was in a shambles. If Dhritarashtra had sent word to the Pandavas — especially to Dharma — 'Take the kingdom, but spare the only son remaining to me,' Dharma could not have refused. He probably would have had to give Duryodhana a small portion of the kingdom as well. As long as both father and son were alive, the Pandavas' claim to the kingdom would never be undisputed. Duryodhana was trying to gain time. The Pandavas, on their side, were trying to find Duryodhana and kill him before any message could come from Dhritarashtra.

While Ashvatthama and Duryodhana were talking loudly, some hunters had come into the vicinity. These people were under Bhima's patronage. Because Bhima was fond of meat and paid well for it, they hunted and sent fresh meat to the camp every day. They had seen the Pandavas and Panchalas returning from their unsuccessful attempt to find Duryodhana, and had overheard the Pandavas asking each other, 'Where could he be hiding?' Later, when they overheard the conversation near the pool, they realized that Duryodhana was hiding there. 'Bhima will pay us far more for this news than for any meat,' they told each other. They ran to the Pandavas' camp and revealed the hiding place of Duryodhana. With great shouts, the Pandavas remounted their chariots and started towards the pool. Hearing their shouts and the noise of their chariots, Duryodhana went back into the pool, and the three warriors ran deep into the forest. Ashvatthama, who a few moments before had been boasting of how he would kill the Pandavas, had run away at the very sound of their approach.

Since his father's death Ashvatthama had been talking of revenge. He had been fuming for three days, but had not been able to kill Dhrishtadyumna. Obviously, he could not face him in a direct combat. Ashvatthama had caused the death of Duryodhana, for whom he professed such concern. Impatient and thoughtless, as soon as he had found out Duryodhana's whereabouts, he had rushed to the pool and stood outside, arguing loudly in broad daylight. Thus he had betrayed the hiding place to the Pandavas. When the Pandavas came, instead of standing by the side of his king, he had run away.

Duryodhana had to come out of the pool against his wish. Flinging insults at him, and prodding him like a snake in a hole, the Pandavas forced him out. Swinging his mace Bhima felled him with a blow on the thigh. He kicked him on the head. Dharma intervened to save Duryodhana from further indignities. In great haste, Dharma sent Krishna to console Dhritarashtra and tell him, 'Do not be angry with us, forgive us. We also are yours'. While Krishna was talking with the two old people, more messengers arrived. From their talk, Krishna suspected that some treachery was afoot. He cut short his visit and hurried back. Taking the Pandavas, Draupadi, and Satyaki out of the crowded camp of the Pandavas, he brought them for the night to the deserted Kaurava camp. The sun went down and it was a dark night.

Krishna had suspected some treachery, but he did not quite know what. That treachery was Ashvatthama's. After leaving Duryodhana, the three warriors were constantly taking note of what was happening. They saw the Pandavas and Panchalas going away and heard the shouts of victory in the Pandava camp. They slipped back to where Duryodhana was. Duryodhana lay mortally wounded on the bank of the pool. Seeing the great king lying in the dust, brought down by Bhima's unfair blow, their hearts were wrung with pity. Ashvatthama swore he would avenge the king as well as his father; and even in Duryodhana's extremity, he had him anoint him a general. If one remembers the pomp and dignity with which the other generals were anointed, this last ceremony seems contemptible. One feels that the poor dying king must have performed the ritual just to free himself of the importunities of Ashvatthama. As soon as he was anointed, Ashvatthama left the king and went away.

After leaving Duryodhana, Ashvatthama and his companions went far into the forest to avoid being found by the Pandava soldiers. Kripa and Kritavarma slept, but Ashvatthama could not sleep. Drona's death had deprived him not only of a father, but of a kingdom. He grieved for Duryodhana, but much more for his own bereavement and loss. Just then he saw a big bat pounce on and kill some sleeping crows. This scene gave him the idea of attacking the Pandavas in their sleep. He woke up Kripa and Kritavarma and told them of his inspiration. Kripa tried his best to dissuade him from this base plan. In this exchange, one sentence of Ashvatthama is especially significant. He told his uncle, 'You tell me to act like a Brahman, but I have never learned the Brahman code. From childhood onwards, all I have learned is weaponry. I was born in a high Brahman family, but unlucky that I am, I have lived as a Kshatriya. Now let me follow that dharma.' Paying no attention to Kripa's objections, he yoked his horse to the chariot and set off at full gallop for the

Pandavas' camp. Wondering what would happen, Kripa and Kritavarma followed him. While Ashvatthama entered the camp, they stood outside. Ashvatthama first went to the sleeping Dhrishtadyumna, woke him and killed him. Then he killed the five sleeping sons of Draupadi. Not knowing who or how many were attacking, everyone in the camp ran helter-skelter. In the meantime, Kripa and Kritavarma set fire to the camp, redoubling the confusion. After he had killed as many as he could, Ashvatthama came out. He hurried with the news to Duryodhana, who rejoiced at it before he died. Then, knowing that the Pandavas and Krishna would be after him for revenge, he ran away again and went to the hut of Vyasa on the banks of the Ganga. The Pandavas followed him. Ashvatthama hurled a terrible magical weapon at Arjuna. Arjuna countered with an equally powerful weapon. The weapons met and as their dual powers were released, the world was about to be destroyed. Vyasa stood at the point of impact and appealed to both of them to recall their weapons. Arjuna, being a true Kshatriya, could call his weapon back but Ashvatthama was unable to do so. The story says that the weapon did not kill the Pandavas, but it did destroy the child in Uttara's womb. The Pandavas allowed Ashvatthama to live. Krishna said he would revive Uttara's dead child, and then he cursed Ashvatthama, 'You will live for thousands of years. You will wander ceaselessly through forests and deserts. No living man will shelter you.' All the other generals had died as warriors. Ashvatthama alone was doomed to a life more terrible than death.

In our philosophy, *smriti* (memory, consciousness) and *moha* (confusion) have a great importance and a special meaning. The Gita's description of the chain of causality ending in man's destruction is well-known: 'Anger leads to loss of consciousness, loss of consciousness brings about confusion in memory, which leads, in its turn, to the loss of thinking power. And the loss of thinking power destroys a person.' From childhood to death, the one thread that creates the oneness in a man's ever-changing life is smriti. Smriti is the power which enables a man to have the ever-present consciousness of who he is and the knowledge that he is the same person from moment to moment. It is because of smriti that a man understands what his duties are, and where he is going. In the Mahabharata, the question 'Who am I?' is bound up with the question, 'What is my place?' Thus the answer to the question of a man's duty too is dependent on the place he holds. Extraordinary people like Krishna and Buddha remember all their former births, and thus reach a oneness not possible for ordinary beings. The ordinary man must try to keep the thread of smriti unbroken at least for this one life. The stress on remaining conscious up to the moment of death is based on this conviction. This is the reason the Gita says one should die in full consciousness, in broad daylight, when the sun is in the north and the moon is waxing. The great effort was not to give in to darkness, not to lose smriti on any account. Bhishma's smriti remained unimpaired all his life. Arjuna was confused as to his duty, but Krishna reminded him of what he was. Waking to the cruel necessity of his duty, Arjuna said, 'Now my confusion is gone, I have regained my smriti.' Drona never had that burning consciousness of his own dharma. As for Ashvatthama, he had completely forgotten himself. He had given up his own dharma and could never understand the dharma of others. He was born a Brahman. He could have become a king because his father had acquired a kingdom. He had learned the use of terrible weapons, but he did not use them to bring victory to Duryodhana; after everything had been lost, he used them only for his own revenge and safety. He had rejected his Brahmanhood, and could never manage to become a Kshatriya. He is the unforgettable example of the loss of smriti.

9 Karna

No one achieves complete success in life; but even partial fulfilment is attained by but a few. Unfulfilment, the Mahabharata tells us again and again, is the normal condition of man. Dharma, after defeating all his enemies said, 'This victory does not feel like victory at all.' To some extent each major figure in the Mahabharata is defeated by life, but none so completely as Karna. Vidura's life resembled Karna's in many respects, but the few aspects in which it did not, made for all the difference in the two characters. Dhritarashtra, Pandu, and Vidura had a common father. But the mothers of the first two were princesses and so each of them, inspite of some physical deformity, could enjoy the throne. Vidura was sound in limb and mind and yet because he was the son of a suta woman, he became a suta too and was deprived of a kingdom. Evidence of his immense frustration and his constant efforts to master it by deep contemplation is found everywhere in the Mahabharata. His birth determined his position in society and so he could devote his energies to transcending his humble earthly personality on another plane. Karna's defeat lay in just this one fact that he did not know who he was by birth; and when the answer was given to him, it was too late.

All through life one is constantly asking, and answering the question: 'Who am I?' This 'I' remains dynamic and changeful; and so at no given moment is a final answer possible. Small children, to start with, often refer to themselves in the third person. The awareness of 'me' is linked with the awareness of 'mine'. This is my mother, my father, my toys, my house, and ultimately the 'I' emerges as the centre of all these possessions. This awareness becomes sharpened through families and social relationships. As the boundaries of the 'I' broaden, the 'I' comes in contact with the 'not I', the 'you' or the 'he', and also their expectations regarding the 'I'. And these are the expectations which shape the various manifestations of the 'I'. One plays different roles as a son, a husband, a father, a citizen, a member of a caste and of a society. Social behaviour and ritual define and limit the identity of the 'I' in his various roles. Vidura was a suta from his very birth and had received all the important life-rituals of a suta. His social position was fixed once and for all. Dhritarashtra called him 'brother', seated him on his knee and embraced him (3.720; also 3.74 and 3.84) but nobody offered him a princess in marriage, nor was he honoured as a Kshatriya. In spite of his social inferiority he was never in any doubt as to who he was. Karna was caught in the vicious grip of this question. He had no definite position in society. He struggled all his life to gain what he thought was his rightful status and his bitterness lay in not having got it.

He had grown up in the house of a suta, Adhiratha. Though Adhiratha and his wife Radha brought him up as their own son, they had not hidden it from him that he was not born to them. He had heard of how he had been found in a box with gold and the earrings and the armour of a Kshatriya. Even the name Vasusena given to him by Adhiratha, was one found only among Kshatriyas. He was ever hopeful that being a Kshatriya by birth, his real parents would some day acknowledge him. Though he dearly loved his foster-parents, he was not prepared to spend his life among them as a suta.

As a suta, he was not allowed to train in weaponry. We are told that to be accepted as a pupil he had to go disguised as a Brahman. When it was accidentally revealed that he was not a Brahman, his teacher cursed him saying that he would forget everything he had learned. The story is obviously a later interpolation, since his alleged teacher Parashurama had lived centuries earlier. The story probably does indicate, however, that education in all the arts of war was open only to Brahmans and Kshatriyas, and that despite this, Karna had managed to attain some excellence in these arts. He took the chance to exhibit his extraordinary skill in warlike arts, but the attempt ended in a disaster. The Pandavas and the Kauravas had finished their studies with Drona. He had arranged for them to exhibit their skills in front of the court. There was a big arena in the middle, and pavilions built around it for people to sit. Dhritarashtra, Gandhari, Kunti, Vidura, Bhishma and all the other elders of the family had come to witness and admire the children's skill. Arjuna excelled among all and astonished everyone with his extraordinary archery. Just then, there was some disturbance at the entrance and a strongly built, handsome youth entered and told the assembled people, 'I can do all that Arjuna has done,' and proceeded to demonstrate. After showing that he was Arjuna's equal in archery, he challenged Arjuna to a duel. This youth was Karna, who till then was unknown to the court. Like all the key-incidents in the Mahabharata, this too is small, fast-moving and dramatic. It ends before one is well aware of what is happening. Not a single person there had any inkling of how this would develop and yet what did happen was of great importance from the point of view of the story. It adds an edge to the conflict and gives new meaning to what follows.

Drona had planned to exhibit the skills of his pupils. No outsiders were invited. And yet Karna entered uninvited. Adhiratha had no idea of this plan. Perhaps Karna came with the hope that after seeing his prowess, his Kshatriya parents might acknowledge him. This object he could have gained by showing that he was as good as the best of them, he need not have challenged Arjuna to a duel. This again raises the question of the relative ages of the princes. If at that time Dharma was about sixteen, Arjuna must have been only about fourteen. Even if Dharma had been eighteen, that still makes Arjuna only sixteen. Karna was Kunti's son born before her marriage, that is, at least two years older than Dharma, perhaps more, so he was four years older than Arjuna. At the ages of sixteen and twenty the physical differences are great. A sixteen-year-old is a boy, whereas a twenty-year-old is nearly an adult. Therefore, Karna should not have challenged a mere boy to a duel. But Karna in the heat of anger would invariably do the things he ought not to. This characteristic weakness of his can be seen again and again in the story. To be rash was a Kshatriya characteristic, but the unwritten rule that one must never be small-minded was broken often by Karna. This failure was due to the peculiar turn his life had taken. He had acquired the skills of the Kshatriyas but he could not master their value-frame. He was obsessed by bitterness at the thought that he was an illegitimate son of a Kshatriya. According to the rules of those times, he could have attained Kshatriyahood in spite of his illegitimacy under certain conditions, but in his case this door was closed to him. He was not fighting on behalf of the suta class nor was he fighting for the idea that Kshatriyahood should be awarded to one who is a valiant warrior. This was not a class war; he was struggling on behalf of his own individual self. In his attempt in the arena to gain recognition he failed. The secret of his birth remained. This only added to his anger. When he issued the challenge to Arjuna, the princes in the arena split into two parties. Bhishma with Dharma and his brothers stood behind Arjuna. Duryodhana with his brothers stood behind Karna. Kripa, who was the hereditary teacher at the court of Hastinapura, knew the code of duelling. He announced, according to custom, 'This is Arjuna, son of Pandu, who accepts the challenge. Unknown challenger warrior, tell us your name and familiy.' Karna stood mute with tears in his eyes. Duryodhana spoke up and said, 'A warrior doesn't need to pronounce his ancestry. If Arjuna is unwilling to fight anyone who is not a king, I shall give the kingdom of Anga to Karna.' And forthwith crowned him. (All this seems to be a later interpolation for the following reasons: Duryodhana at the time was a prince. His father was on the throne while Bhishma administered the kingdom. That the possibility of Dharma getting the kingdom had arisen is clear in the next chapter. In these circumstances, Duryodhana could never have given any kingdom to Karna. And performing the elaborate ritual of crowning Karna on the spot was quite impossible. Barring this incident, the things that happened later were consistent and inevitable.) Kripa asked Karna to announce his name and family and we have seen that he stood mute with tears in his eyes. Just then there was a commotion at the door again. Adhiratha, who had heard where Karna had gone, entered in a great hurry, hardly able to walk in his agitation. On seeing him, Karna went to him and bowing with respect called him 'Father' and Adhiratha embraced him as his son. Thus was Kripa answered. Not only was Karna's hope of gaining Kshatriyahood shattered, but his suta origin was also publicly proclaimed. Bhima took the opportunity to rub salt in the wound: 'You should hold a whip to suit your trade and not a sword.' Duryodhana embraced Karna and offered him his friendship which was accepted gratefully. By this time the sun went down. And thus ended both the quarrels and the exhibition of prowess at arms.

Instead of getting an answer to the nagging question: 'Who am I?' Karna was led into greater confusion. If not then, at some later date he did become the king of Anga, and yet he seems always to have been at the court of the Kauravas. His friendship with Duryodhana did not bring him a higher social rank nor did it enable him to reach equality with the Kshatriyas. In spite of the declaration of friendship, Duryodhana never offered a girl from the Kaurava family as a bride to Karna. As Karna himself has said in *Udyogaparva,* not only he but his children also had married into suta families. The very circumstances which led to this friendship were such that a relationship of equality could never be established. Karna always remained a trusted and close retainer. He was tied to Duryodhana more out of gratitude than affection. The more firmly his low birth became established in public the more certain he was inwardly of his Kshatriya origins. This caused him terrible mental agony. He did not know that he was in any way related to the Pandavas. The hatred he acquired for them could have the following reasons: Bhima as we saw had wounded and insulted him wantonly; he was jealous of Arjuna's reputation as the greatest archer of his times; and to add to this he had accepted the friendship of Duryodhana who was a sworn enemy of the Pandavas. Unfortunately, he proved inferior in this first encounter, and the envy and hatred grew in his heart. Even later on, whenever Karna and Arjuna met, Karna could not prove himself to be either a better warrior or a better man.

At the time of Draupadi's marriage, Arjuna alone

among all the assembled people could perform the difficult feat which won her hand.[1] Arjuna at that time was in the guise of a Brahman. All the Kshatriyas were incensed that a Kshatriya princess should be won by a Brahman and so they fell on him. A skirmish took place with Bhima and Arjuna on one side and all the others including Karna on the other. The two succeeded in fighting off the others. We are told that Karna withdrew from battle after a while, saying that he would not fight Brahmans. As he was having the worse of the encounter, this sounds merely like an excuse to save face.

The incident of the dice game tested everybody: the sightless Dhritarashtra avid for news, asking every minute, 'What's happening, what's going on?' Duhshasana, dancing with delight, crying 'gow-gow' at the moment of triumph; Vidura striving to save Draupadi's honour; all were tested. And so was Karna who, though an outsider, took part in the family quarrel and proved himself the meanest of them all. Dharma, after having lost everything else at dice, had staked his own freedom and that of his brothers and wife. He lost that too. Draupadi was dragged to the court and a dispute arose as to whether she really was a slave or not. A younger brother of Duryodhana, Vikarna, argued on her behalf, saying that it was not seemly to put to shame a gentlewoman in this manner and that she could not be made a slave. Karna stood up in anger and

---

1 A latter addition has it that Karna had risen to attempt the feat but was rejected by Draupadi on the grounds that he was low-born. This passage has been deleted from the new critical edition.

refuted Vikarna. He said, 'The wife of five husbands is no better than a strumpet. There's nothing wrong in dragging her to the men's assembly. She and her husbands are all nothing but slaves now. They do not own even the clothes they are wearing. Strip them of their finery.' On hearing this, the Pandavas immediately took off their upper garments. And Duhshasana started to disrobe Draupadi at Karna's instigation. Karna alone induced the Kauravas to degrade Draupadi, for until he spoke none had thought of it. The quarrel over the division of the kingdom was between men. It could be solved as they pleased by war or by dice. There was no reason to thus dishonour the wife of the defeated men. Here it was not a question of Karna's high or low birth. Nor was it a point of legal niceties. It was a simple question of whether one should dishonour a well-born woman under any circumstances. He had no cause to take part in the quarrel between the cousins. He not only participated in it, but became so involved that he showed that under stress he could forget all humane considerations.

At the time of the *ghoshayatra* (cattle-inspection) Karna was once again found wanting; this time as a warrior. In those days kings had large herds of cattle, which were kept in pastures near the borders of the kingdom. These pastures were generally surrounded by forests which was a no-man's land between two kingdoms. Once in a while the king would visit the herds and see that the new calves were branded with his symbol. Soon after the dice game, Duryodhana planned to visit his herds along with Duhshasana and

Karna. The Pandavas in their exile were living in the forest near the pastures. Duryodhana went with great pomp, accompained by the women of the family, slaves and retainers in a number of chariots, exhibiting the newly acquired riches of the Kaurava court. The inspection of the herds was only a pretence. The real object of the visit was to exhibit the ill-gotten gains of the Kauravas before the Pandavas, living in the forest in poverty. At this time, a quarrel broke out between Duryodhana and a people called Gandharvas who also had come there picknicking. The Gandharvas gave a sound drubbing to the Kauravas and took Duryodhana prisoner. In this skirmish, Karna had to run away and hide in a nearby village. Ultimately, the Pandavas came to the rescue of Duryodhana, freed him and sent him back to Hastinapura. But before that, the news of his imprisonment had reached Hastinapura, and Bhishma had started with an army to rescue the king. On the way, the news of the rescue also reached him. Just then Karna met him and asked after the king. Bhishma answered angrily, 'Those loyal to the king don't live to ask whether the king be alive. How could you think of your own hide with the king in danger? Your much vaunted love for the king is nothing but a pretence.' Until then Karna had thought of himself as Duryodhana's friend. But this incident and Bhishma's cruel comment put him in his place and did not allow him even the illusion of friendship. Once again he had been put to the test and had failed.

The next incident was that of the Kauravas robbing the cattle of Virata. At that time Arjuna was alone against all the Kaurava warriors. Even then Karna could not withstand Arjuna. It is said that Arjuna not only defeated all, but also robbed them of their clothes which he gave to Virata's daughter for her doll. Even if this is an exaggeration, there is no doubt that he did succeed in chasing them away and rescuing the cattle that they were stealing. In this battle Arjuna had to make do with a cowardly charioteer but still proved himself superior as a warrior from a chariot against all the Kauravas.

Karna was said to be the son of the Sun-god who, however, plays no decisive role in the story. Karna did not know who his father was for a long time; and yet he worshipped the Sun, one does not know why. The armour and the earrings which he is supposed to have received at birth from the Sun and which had some magic power, he gave to Indra. The rings he tore from his ears. The armour he is supposed to have peeled from his body like skin, and hurt and bloodied himself. One cannot understand this. In each battle which is described, Karna wore his armour. This stripping away or 'peeling' of a 'natural armour' did not prevent him from wearing armour. Nor did the 'natural armour' give him any extra advantage as is seen in all the above incidents where he was defeated. Why did Karna have this urge to show such extreme generosity to Indra? Was this due to the insecurity he felt about his own position? Did he want to prove himself better than the Kshatriyas? As we have already seen, he tended to go to extremes both in his evil deeds as well as in his good ones.

There were, however, a few golden moments in his

otherwise sad life. These were not moments of great joy, achievement or honour. Outwardly he remained what he was. Those were the moments when he could have felt fulfilled because then he came to know who he was. This knowledge posed a dilemma from which he extricated himself nobly. All through his life he is a confused person, but on these two occasions his thoughts and actions were clear and decisive. He was never in doubt as to what to do. All turbidity had vanished and his mind was crystal clear. The first of these incidents was when Krishna asked him to join the Pandavas, and the second was when Kunti told him that she was his mother. After telling him that he was Kunti's eldest son and as such the eldest brother of the Pandavas, Krishna promised Karna all that Karna had ever desired in his life and more. By accepting Krishna's offer, he would have become at once a Kshatriya of the highest rank and a king. The Pandavas, his hated rivals, would have waited on him as their eldest. All this he gave up, and easily, without saying one harsh word to Krishna. He said, 'What you ask is impossible. My whole life has been spent among the sutas, and I and my sons have married among them. I cannot now break away from them. Any kingdom that I win I would present to Duryodhana. Do not try to persuade me.' 'So be it,' said Krishna and turned away. This shows Karna to be a noble person, a true friend, a man tied to his foster family by love and duty, an incorruptible vassal. The second incident was his conversation with Kunti. He spoke with extreme bitterness but never showed smallness of mind. She met him on the banks of the

Ganges when he was worshipping the Sun-god. After finishing the ritual, he turned to her and asked her what she wanted. She told him the history of his birth, and said, 'So, you are the brother of the Pandavas. Come over to their side. Let the world see the great powers of the brothers Karna and Arjuna. You are not a suta. Become famous as a warrior.' Karna said, 'If you expect my troubles to be over simply because you have revealed to me the secret of my birth, you are mistaken. Your story establishes me as a Kshatriya, but in name only, because I have never received the rituals due to a Kshatriya. The first ritual I should have received at birth, but then you abandoned me ruthlessly. You come to me now only through selfish motives. Anyone would fear Arjuna helped by Krishna. Now if I desert the Kauravas, it would be imputed to my fear of Arjuna. Duryodhana has plunged into this battle on the strength of my support. I can never do what you ask. I will not kill any of your other sons but Arjuna. If Arjuna kills me you have your five sons and if I kill him, you will still have five counting me.' Kunti managed to say, 'Keep your word then,' and went away.

There is no meanness in this answer, yet his offer to kill none but Arjuna would not stand up to examination. On its face it looks like generosity. It seems like one of the exaggerated gestures he was so fond of making. But it was not so. He had neither love nor pity for Kunti. He was equally indifferent to his so-called brothers. When he said that he would not kill the others, it was not generosity or love which prompted him, but extreme contempt. The meaning of his promise was that he would engage with the one he thought his equal. He was not concerned with the others. This contempt and overconfidence was not misplaced in a Kshatriya. But it was certainly not appropriate in this context. This was a real war, not a tournament. It was his duty to help Duryodhana win the war and not engage in an empty boast. He was hurting Duryodhana's cause in promising not to kill the others, especially Dharma. It has to be said that he ignored Duryodhana's need and was carried away by a false notion of his own greatness.

This incident revealed to him who he really was. However, since he could not play the role befitting his new identity, he rejected it. But at least in private he should have felt free of the burden of uncertainty which he had carried all his life. By spurning for the sake of his friend what he had coveted always, he attained moral grandeur. This one moment should have brought fulfilment to him, but in the remaining few weeks of life he fell into the old rut. His own actions brought about his downfall and the others too did not spare him.

Just before the battle opened Bhishma enumerated the names of the *maharathi* who were the most highly accomplished fighters from chariots and those who had only half the qualities. He put Karna in the second category because of his impulsiveness. This evaluation had nothing to do with Karna's social status; it referred directly to his individual, personal shortcoming. Though Karna was annoyed by it, the truth of Bhishma's judgment of him was borne out by the events in the Mahabharata. A *rathi* (warrior) used to fight standing in a *rath* (chariot). He also knew how to drive a chariot. Krishna, Arjuna and Bhishma knew both, fighting and driving. Karna grew up among hereditary charioteers, but seems to have never driven a chariot, He only fought from a chariot. It was apparently necessary to know the finer points of chariot driving in order to be able to shoot arrows effectively from a moving chariot. The outcome of this quarrel between Bhishma and Karna was that Karna refused to fight as long as Bhishma was in command and thus was out of the battle for full nine days. There again we see how he always put his own pride before the good of Duryodhana, his friend.[1] Drona too fully agreed with Bhishma's judgment of Karna as a chariot warrior. 'Karna is headstrong, shows misplaced kindness, runs away from battle and makes mistakes in judgment. And so I would not give him full marks as a warrior.' Drona was the best instructor in warfare in his day. This criticism should have made Karna pause to think. If only he had thought, he would have realised that though possessed of ability, he could not obtain good training. He would have been forced to admit his limitations. But he was not given to self-examination.

After Bhishma's fall, Karna came out on the battlefield. The army demanded that he be made the general. He, too, came there in a great chariot. But he

---

1 The other version of this incident says that it was Bhishma who refused to fight if Karna was allowed to take part in the battle. It seems very peculiar that Duryodhana should have agreed to such a stipulation.

himself advised Duryodhana to offer the generalship to Drona, who would be acceptable to all. Drona fought for three days and destroyed a great number of enemy warriors. Karna did not get a chance to meet Arjuna face to face. On the other hand, one of his best weapons had to be used against some other warrior. It was during these three days that Arjuna's sixteen-year-old son was surrounded and killed by six or seven warriors all together, Karna amongst them. When the boy's chariot broke, he had jumped down and fought these renowned warriors standing on the ground alone. After the death of Drona, Karna became the general, on the sixteenth day of the battle. By then, though both sides had lost heavily, the Pandavas had a slight advantage. Ashvatthama, the son of Drona, advised Duryodhana to make truce, but Duryodhana was depending on Karna. He felt that Karna could do what none else had done. Nothing remarkable happened on the first day. The next day Karna asked that Shalya, the King of Madra, become his chariot driver. Shalya said that he was a great king and a Kshatriya, and that he would rather leave the battle and return to his kingdom than drive the chariot of a low-born person. With great difficulty Duryodhana persuaded him to do the service. Then Karna went to the battlefield with Shalya driving the chariot. Before reaching the field, a long conversation took place between the two. This part seems to be an interpolation because there are in it sentiments completely foreign to the Mahabharata. Shalya said, 'Don't boast now, for I know that you shall lose heart on seeing Arjuna.' Though taunts of this sort were usually offered to warriors in order to rouse their anger,[1] Karna misunderstood them, went off at a tangent and started abusing Shalya and his country. He said that the women of Madra, Shalya's country, were immoral, drank wine and ate beef. He threatened to kill Shalya and accused him of moral turpitude. This conversation, though finding a place in the present critical edition, must be treated as a later addition. Shalya was the crowned king of Madra. The princesses of Madra (each called Madri) had been married into the house of Hastinapura for generations. Besides Shalya, there was another prince of Madra, a cousin of Duryodhana, also fighting for the Kauravas. No matter how impetuous Karna was, he should never have insulted in such terms a close and exalted relative of Duryodhana. All the Kshatriya men and women of those times drank freely; it is also probable that beef-eating was common. The prohibition against drinking and beef-eating belongs to a much later age and is out of place here.

After Karna's outburst, Shalya stopped talking. Karna ordered that white horses be yoked to his chariot, perhaps to imitate Arjuna. This was foolish because it is well-known that one had one's own trusted charioteer, well-trained and familiar horses and a chariot to which one was accustomed. In a battle as critical as the one he was about to face, he should have held to this principle.

---

1 Krishna had similarly taunted Arjuna, whose chariot he drove. This was done not in order to discourage a warrior but to rouse him to greater anger and to make him perform better in battle. The passages which suggest otherwise are, therefore, thought by the author to be later additions.

He already had a strange charioteer in Shalya, and now he also ordered new horses. One is forced to say that the very first step he took in an important battle was a false one. He had, as was customary, another chariot accompanying him, filled with arrows and other weapons. He went through the Kauravas' ranks shouting loudly: 'Show Arjuna to me. Where is he? I cannot see him. Hasn't anybody seen him?' And yet he did not immediately face Arjuna even though Arjuna, Bhima and their brother-in-law Dhrishtadyumna were destroying the Kaurava warriors in great number. After some time, Shalya pointed out Arjuna's chariot. 'Now is the time to repay all the kindness that Duryodhana has shown you,' he said, and drove the chariot towards Arjuna. As Karna approached him, he saw his son Vrishasena attacking Arjuna, and Arjuna killed him before Karna could do anything. Karna had fallen silent by now and it was Arjuna who was shouting in the fury of battle. Karna's eyes filled with tears to see his son killed but he dashed them away and faced Arjuna. A battle ensued. Gradually Arjuna gained, Karna was streaming with blood, his armour had broken. As a desperate measure, Karna brought out an arrow with a 'cobra sitting on it'. (This may mean that the arrow was poisoned with snake venom and would kill the victim even if it succeeded in breaking the skin anywhere.) He aimed. Shalya said that the aim was wrong if he meant to pierce Arjuna's throat. But Karna would not listen, and tightened the string. He missed by about half a foot and struck Arjuna's coronet instead. There is another conflicting version which says that when Krishna saw the arrow coming, he made the horses bend their knees and brought Arjuna's chariot twenty-four inches lower. The editor thinks that this version is of a later origin when every incident was twisted in order to bring out Krishna's greatness. The author agrees with this because if the chariot had been lowered by as much as twenty-four inches the arrow would have sailed over the chariot and would not have hit Arjuna's coronet. It is more plausible that Karna missed his mark by a mere six inches. He must have already lost his nerve by witnessing the death of his son. On top of it he missed his aim which added to his confusion and then the last straw was that his chariot skidded and the wheel got stuck in the earth. This was the seventeenth day of the battle. The corpses of men, horses and elephants lay rotting, entangled in the broken remains of the chariots. The soft, water-logged earth of northern India had become wet and slippery. It was but natural that his chariot should have skidded and stuck. Every day of the battle the chariots broke or the horses were killed and the warriors transferred to other chariots. And yet Karna jumped down and tried to free the heavy wheel from the mud. It was not possible for one man to do it, and that too in the thick of the battle. One wonders why Karna did not change his chariot. As the day was drawing to a close, the fighting was about to stop for the night. Perhaps Karna had expected to gain a short respite by this ruse. There is no doubt that by this time he was badly rattled. He begged of Arjuna: 'Do not fight me now while I am releasing the wheel. You know the code of battle. A man from a chariot must not fight a man on foot. Fight according to the dharma of battle.'

Krishna had no intention of letting him off. His use of the word 'dharma' gave Krishna the weapon for his destruction. It was not Karna now who asked himself 'Who am I?' Krishna's questions posed the same problem. 'Did you remember this dharma when you incited Duhshasana to strip Draupadi? Did you remember your dharma when the six of you in your chariots killed the boy Abhimanyu standing alone on the ground?'

Krishna was the one who induced the unwilling Arjuna to fight by reminding him of his duty. That very Krishna now at the time of Karna's death stripped him completely of self-esteem. What Krishna meant to say was: why should Karna expect any mercy or justice when he had shown none either to Draupadi or to Abhimanyu.[1] These questions showed that Karna had no right to demand justice. On the other hand, they reminded Arjuna of two great wrongs he had suffered at Karna's hands. He thought: this is the man who shamed my wife. This is the man who ruthlessly killed my boy. He started up with hatred and putting an arrow to the string bellowed, 'May this arrow take Karna's life and prove me to be a true Kshatriya.' Arjuna was famous for not missing his mark. Neither did he this time.

---

1 In later editions there are additional questions which show that those who made the additions did not understand the point of the situation at all.

Karna enters the Mahabharata first at the time of the tournaments. In a way what happened then was re-enacted in this his last appearance. Then he was asked by Kripa, 'Who are you?' And he had to hang his head in shame without an answer. The last scene was a real battle. The duel he had demanded at that time, he now had the chance to fight. This was not make-believe. In this battle, no quarter was given by any party. There were no alternatives to killing or being killed. Karna was facing his life-long enemy whom he had envied and hated. He should never have asked for any consideration from him. Once again Karna did what he ought never to have done. He begged for fair play. And this time it was Krishna who asked him, 'What right have you to expect fair play?' And Karna died without finding an answer to what he was and what his rights were.

10 Krishna Vasudeva

Krishna enters the story of the Mahabharata at the very end of *Adiparva*, the first part, at the time of the marriage of Draupadi. Before this he is in no way involved with either the Kauravas or the Pandavas. Pandu had married Kunti, Vasudeva's sister (Krishna's aunt). Beyond this one mention, even the house of the Yadavas is not referred to. While the Pandavas were growing up, they survived many attempts on their lives, mainly owing to the ceaseless vigilance of Kunti and Vidura. But during all these hard times Kunti never seems to have sought the help of her parental house, the Yadavas. Gandhari's brother, on the one hand, had established himself firmly at the Kaurava court from the day of his sister's marriage to Dhritarashtra. On the other hand, Kunti's and Madri's people are not even heard of. Perhaps they did attend the weddings but returned immediately as was customary. Once her husband had died and she herself was placed in the lowly position of a dependant at the Kaurava court, Kunti could not expect anyone from her father's home to come and willingly share her own indignity. Certainly, she and her fatherless children would have found a home with the Yadavas, but she feared that their absence from Hastinapura would endanger their claim to the throne. Even today, a wise widow would thus live humbly in her brother-in-law's house so as not to jeopardise her son's right to the ancestral property. Also, the Yadavas themselves were busy during this very period. Krishna had killed Kamsa and as a result made an enemy of the powerful monarch Jarasandha, Kamsa's father-in-law. Jarasandha succeeded in driving the Yadavas out of their home on the banks of the Jamuna. The Yadavas fled south to Gujarat and established the new city of Dvaraka on the seashore and regained their former status. These might have been the various reasons why the Yadavas are not heard of in the story until the time of the Pandavas' marriage. Krishna and Balarama had come there not to win Draupadi but to be present at an important Kshatriya gathering. As soon as Krishna saw Arjuna getting up from among the Brahmans and performing the difficult feat of archery that won the princess, he recognised all the five brothers who, his spies had told him, had not died in the fire at Varanavata. When he saw Dharma leave the assembly, he followed him home, greeted Kunti and went back immediately to Dvaraka, whence he returned with many Yadavas, bearing rich presents for the marriage ceremony. After this first meeting, most of the major successes of the Pandavas were achieved with the help of Krishna. The Pandavas had gained the alliance of the house of Drupada by their marriage. The Yadavas, too, openly acknowledged them as kinsfolk and friends. With two such powerful allies, the Pandavas could not be denied their right to the kingdom of Hastinapura. Dhritarashtra, realising this, made over to them the town of Khandavaprastha and the surrounding forest area. The Pandavas with Krishna's help burnt the forest, brought new land under the plough, enlarged the small town to become their capital, the city of Indraprastha. After settling them there, Krishna went back to Dvaraka. Many people, including learned Brahmans, came to Dharma's new capital and gave him the idea of performing the Rajasuya yajna performed by kings. This sacrifice, if performed succesfully, establishes the superiority of the king over all his contemporaries. In order to accomplish it, a king has to have a core of strong kin-group, personal popularity and some other friendly kings who are willing to agree to his suzerainty. There still remain a few who have to be conquered in battle. The preparations for the sacrifice began by 'conquering expeditions' in all directions, east, west, north and south. As usual Krishna was called for consultations. He showed his knowledge and political acumen by telling Dharma the names of kings on whom he could rely as allies and others whom he would have to defeat. He also recalled the rout of the Yadavas at the hands of Jarasandha, king of Magadha, and convinced Dharma that this powerful monarch would have to be subdued before the Rajasuya could even be thought of. This is one of the few places where we hear from Krishna himself some details of his early life. Apart from this, the Mahabharata says nothing at all of his childhood and boyhood in Vrindavana and Mathura as do the later Puranas, *Harivamsha* and *Bhagavata*. From the Mahabharata we know that many Yadava clans like Vrishni, Andhaka, Bhoja and others had settled in Dvaraka, apparently under the rule of Balarama, Krishna's eldest half-brother. Many great Yadava warriors are mentioned time and again. We know their clan and parentage, but even if every scrap of information given there is gathered together, it is not possible to construct a connected account and genealogy. It seems from their descriptions that they were rich, strong, quick-tempered, ready to sport their weapons at the smallest provocation, proud, and very skilful charioteers. They possessed enormous riches. There were factions amongst them. One party wanted Krishna to be their king, but he had many opponents too. So, in order to avoid all internal strife, Krishna crowned Balarama, the eldest son of his father, king. There was never any open quarrel between the two, yet they had many differences on important matters. Balarama must have been aware that his position was due mainly to Krishna, and he had to agree to his wishes on some occasions. Arjuna abducted and married Subhadra, their half-sister, with Krishna's knowledge and help. Balarama with the other Yadava heroes were bent on pursuing Arjuna and bringing her back, but Krishna succeeded in convincing them about the desirability of an alliance with the Pandavas. Krishna was especially fond of the Pandavas. Though Balarama wished them well, he was not partial to them as against the Kauravas who, too, were the cousins of the Yadavas. In the war, he remained neutral. When Bhima hit Duryodhana on the thigh with his mace, against the rules, Balarama wanted to kill Bhima for the foul act but once again Krishna stopped him. The internal factions amongst the Yadavas became apparent at the time of the war. Krishna and his supporters were on the Pandavas' side, whereas many other Yadavas went over to the Kauravas. Like all Kshatriyas of his time Krishna had many wives of whom Satyabhama, the daughter of Satrajit, was the eldest and therefore the most important. She always accompanied Krishna on his visits to the Pandavas. Rukmini, who in later books assumes more importance, is mentioned but once or twice. The Krishna shown in the Mahabharata has no resemblance at all to the flute-playing lover of milkmaids, the divine child, or the miracle-worker of later tradition. It is true that he did win many women, as did his friend Arjuna. But this was not a sign of running after women, it was more a symbol of valour. Marriages among the Kshatriyas were contracted more out of political necessity than love. Of the Pandavas, Arjuna was the same age as Krishna. He always bowed to Dharma and Bhima as his elders, and was, in turn, shown respect by the twins, but he always embraced Arjuna as an equal. These two picknicked together, drank together and were intimate friends. At about this time, the Yadavas had not been long in Dvaraka after very troubled times. The Pandavas, too, for the first time in their life, were enjoying independence and safety. Krishna must have seen that for both the houses the alliance would be very profitable. His personal friendship with Arjuna was, however, a matter of pure affection and deep regard. Krishna's relation with the

Pandavas cannot be understood without reference to his whole life. Though he says in the Gita that he had no ambition or objective at all, yet he had, in reality, many political and personal goals to attain. Some of these goals concerned his clan, some the whole class of Kshatriyas and some were entirely personal. His reason for killing Kamsa was in part personal, in part it was to liberate his clan from a despot. He had to protect his people from Jarasandha and also, after having given security to them, he had to keep them together, repressing their eternal quarrels. Another of his objectives was to kill Jarasandha. This, too, involved the dual purpose of personal revenge and the good of the Kshatriya class. Jarasandha had imprisoned one hundred reigning kings whom he intended to sacrifice to god. This was totally opposed to the Kshatriya code of those times and had upset the internal order of the class. That is why his destruction was essential for the good of the class. The Mahabharata is very explicit about the structure of the Kshatriya society and the strict code of behaviour of the many clans with respect to one another, who were all related and who ruled over the whole of the Gangetic plain. From west to east, the kingdoms of Sindhu, Saumira, Madra, Gandhara, Matsya, Panchala, Hastinapura, Magadha, Chedi and Vidarbha, were ruled by hereditary kings for generations. When the Yadavas left their kingdom of Mathura and founded the new capital of Dvaraka, they do not seem to have wrested it from any reigning king. Many battles and conquests are described, but there is not a single mention of any king being deprived by any other of his kingdom. After Dharma won the Mahabharata battle, Vyasa advised him: 'Send messengers to the kingdoms of all those who have died in battle. Assure the widowed queens of personal safety and crown the young heirs and guard them. If a widow be with child give her protection and when an heir is born, make him the king and appoint reliable guardians (regents).' (*Shantiparva* 34.31-33). All this shows that there was a code of war, and conquering each other's kingdom was not a part of it. The advice that Krishna gave to Dharma at the time of the Rajasuya sacrifice brings this out very vividly. When the four brothers conquered many kings, they took from them tribute and their consent to Dharma's suzerainty, invited them to be guests at the sacrifice and returned. Shishupala too had meant this very thing when he told Dharma, in effect, that the Rajasuya was made possible by the consent of all. Krishna again emphasised this while talking about and to Jarasandha. He said, 'It is against the Kshatriya code that you should imprison kings and plan to sacrifice them. We have no quarrel with you if you release them all.' When Jarasandha would not agree to this, he had to be killed. The performer of the Rajasuya had to prove not only his valour but also his adherence to the Kshatriya dharma. According to Krishna, Dharma, the eldest of the Pandavas, fulfilled both these conditions. Though the Rajasuya sacrifice gave the performer the title of *Samrat* (suzerain king) this did not involve upsetting the Kshatriya order in which kings of nearly equal rank and strength ruled neighbouring kingdoms. Jarasandha's defeating and imprisoning other kings had shaken the very foundation of this order.

It is only from Buddhist times onwards that we get descriptions of empires and empire-builders. Kings endeavoured to annex their neighbours' kingdoms to their own. Such empires were built by the king of Kosala, by Chandragupta Maurya, Ashoka, Samudra Gupta, etc. Kalidas, the great Sanskrit poet, who lived about fifteen hundred years after the Mahabharata war, and belonged to the empire-building era, referred nostalgically to the vanished Kshatriya code of olden days. He wrote about the ancient kings of Ayodhya and said, 'King Raghu deprived the king of Kalinga of his glory but not of his land.' Thus, in the Mahabharata times, the so-called 'world-conquest' was a game played according to strict rules. The objective was to gain fame, not territory. Another rule of the game was to collect wealth in the form of tributes from the conquered kings and to spend it in giving gifts at the time of the sacrifice when the invited kings were feasted for days, honoured with suitable gifts and sent back to their kingdoms. This very idea was mentioned by Kalidasa again when he described how Raghu was reduced to poverty after his Rajasuya. Krishna was endeavouring to re-establish this order of the class and for this the destruction of Jarasandha was necessary.

Knowing that it would be difficult to defeat Jarasandha in a full battle, Krishna had Bhima kill him in single combat. After the killing of Jarasandha, the 'world-conquest' was but a formal affair and Dharma could successfully perform the Rajasuya sacrifice.

On the final day of the sacrifice only one duty remained: to honour the assembled Kshatriyas, giving special recognition to the wisest and the best among them. Dharma naturally chose Krishna for this honour after consulting Bhishma. King Shishupala, Krishna's cousin and rival, objected saying that elders like Bhishma or Vidura should receive the honour. Tension in the pavilion rose as Shishupala spoke. He grossly insulted Bhishma and the Pandavas and started to incite the assembled kings to walk out of the pavilion and challenge the Pandavas to a fight. Such a quarrel would have reduced to nothing a year's ceaseless effort to perform the sacrifice. Before such a dreadful thing could happen, Krishna got up and swiftly threw his discus at Shishupala, severing his head. Though shocked, the assembled kings were unable to take any concerted action. They allowed themselves to be pacified and the Rajasuya drew to a triumphant conclusion. This killing of Shishupala was not premeditated and Krishna has been blamed for it. But if one reads the whole episode one can see that he averted a catastrophe by this timely though ruthless deed. Shishupala had come as an invited guest and ally, but he had forfeited his rights by having transgressed the rules and limits of propriety.

All these efforts of Krishna were on behalf of his family, the Yadavas, his friends the Pandavas, and the whole Kshatriya class. He had, however, also a personal ambition. This ambition was to become a *'Vasudeva'*, a position approaching divinity. The Krishna in the Mahabharata is definitely not a god, as depicted in later literature. He was, however, an extraordinary man, and his great personal ambition was to be called Vasudeva.

Exactly what becoming a Vasudeva means is not made clear in the Mahabharata. Ordinarily Vasudeva would be simply a patronymic: the son of Vasudeva. In that sense, as sons of Vasudeva, Krishna and all his brothers were already Vasudevas. All we know from the Mahabharata is that 'Vasudeva' was apparently a title which could be borne by only one man in an age.

The significance of being a Vasudeva can only be understood from Jain sources. The Jains are known as great systematizers. They have divided the wheel of time into twenty-four sections, during twelve of which the world was supposed to be getting better and better. This period was called the *utsarpini* (upgrade). The remaining was one of regression, called *avasarpini* (downgrade). In one epoch of twenty-four divisions, nine Vasudevas were born. Rama and Krishna both were Vasudevas born in a period of regression.

The significance of being a Vasudeva can only be radiance. The *'Baladeva'* was the brother of the Vasudeva, mainly known for his devotion to the Vasudeva. The *'Prati-Vasudeva'* was the main enemy of the Vasudeva. In the last epoch, Krishna was the Vasudeva, his brother Balarama was the Baladeva, and Jarasandha, the Prati-Vasudeva. In one of the previous epochs these were Rama, Laxmana and Ravana.

The Vasudeva was a ruler of great valour, splendour and of the seven most precious things in the world, and the most beautiful woman. Three more things are said of him: he lacked nothing, he found something good in everything, and he never fought standing on the ground.

The Krishna of the Mahabharata can be said to possess the seven precious things, some of which are mentioned by name in the Mahabharata and all of which are mentioned in the later Puranas. The description of his riches and personal splendour makes it clear that he lacked nothing. He was known as the best charioteer of his times, a warrior who never fought on the ground.

Immediately after the Rajasuya sacrifice, Krishna set out to establish his claim to the title of Vasudeva. He went to Pundra, where the king called himself 'Vasudeva'. Challenging him to combat, Krishna killed him. He came back. He had accomplished everything he wanted for himself, for his friends, his clan, and his class. But to his horror he found that Dharmaraja had lightly gambled away the kingdom which he had won him with such effort.

He did not reprimand Dharma. He only said, 'If I had been here, I would never have allowed this dice game.' While consoling the Pandavas and Draupadi for the loss of the kingdom and their exile in the forest, he promised them that he and the Drupadas would take care of the other queens and the children. In the final year of their exile he went to see them and again reassured them of his friendship, and promised that he would help them regain their kingdom.

A year later, when the Pandavas came out of disguise and declared themselves, their situation was similar to that at the time of Draupadi's swayamvara

Once again, they had just come out of hiding, were without a kingdom, and were arranging a marriage alliance. For, Abhimanyu, the son of Arjuna, was being married to Uttara, the daughter of Virata. Again the friends and allies of the Pandavas assembled: the Yadavas, the Drupadas, and now the Viratas. After a long consultation it was decided to send Krishna to Hastinapura to plead the Pandavas' case. If he could not get Duryodhana to agree to giving back the Pandavas' share of the kingdom, Krishna was empowered to make whatever compromise he thought fit.

Up to the time of the Rajasuya sacrifice, Krishna's main concern was for the political situation of the day. He did, of course, care for his friends, and was an intimate companion of Arjuna. His friendship, however, had been only one part of his many-sided life. But after the Pandavas' exile, he set aside all his other ambitions to devote himself to their cause. The Pandavas were valorous, but they lacked the wisdom to direct their own affairs. Krishna took it upon himself to look after their personal safety, their kingly position, and their reputation as warriors.

He went to Hastinapura and met Duryodhana. Though he tried his utmost to reason with Duryodhana, he could neither bring about a reconciliation nor an honourable compromise. War was inevitable.

Both sides started preparations. To secure allies they visited the neighbouring kings. Duryodhana from Hastinapura and Arjuna from Virata's capital went to Dvaraka to seek the Yadavas' help. Balarama was partial to the Hastinapura house, but he refused to enter the conflict on either side. Kritavarma, from the clan of Hardika, joined the Kauravas. Satyaki and other friends of Krishna, joined the Pandavas. Duryodhana and Arjuna reached Krishna's house at the same time. Krishna was sleeping. Arjuna sat at the foot of the bed, Duryodhana at the head. As soon as Krishna woke, both requested his help. Krishna agreed to help both sides. To one side he would give his famed soldiers, the Narayaniya. On the other side he himself would be present, but would not take up arms. Since on waking he had seen Arjuna first, he gave the choice to him. Arjuna chose Krishna, and Duryodhana, well-satisfied, went away with the army.

Krishna, pleased at Arjuna's confidence and at his request, agreed to be his charioteer. Arjuna had made the right choice. The Pandavas did not lack warriors; what they needed was a dispassionate, determined counsellor. That they found in Krishna.

The very first day of the war all of Krishna's persuasive power was required to make Arjuna fight. Seeing the Kaurava army filled with his kinsmen and led by his grandfather, and his teacher, Arjuna had no heart to fight. In an impulse of revulsion he threw down his weapons. Krishna remonstrated, reminding Arjuna of his duty as a Kshatriya and warning him that he would be called a coward. Arjuna still refused. Krishna continued his argument: 'What finally are you afraid of? You are afraid of killing these people. But everything that lives must die. Just now as a Kshatriya your duty is to kill these people. You refuse to do what is necessary, thinking thereby that you can avoid doing something bad. But once you are born, you are involved in actions. You cannot choose not to act, nor can you always do as you want. Your whole position in life determines the actions you have to perform. Your action is bad only when you do it for what you will gain from it. Therefore act properly, don't think of what you will gain, don't act for specific ends, and never hope to live without acting.' Krishna continued his arguments, stressing that one cannot run away from life: 'You can realize *Brahman* only by fulfilling the duties of your position on earth. Not ascetic retreat, but dispassionate, considered action is the only way to the Absolute.'

Arjuna at last agreed to fight, but refused to stand against Bhishma. In exasperation Krishna leapt from his chariot, whip in hand, to kill Bhisma himself. Arjuna jumped down, embraced Krishna's feet, and begged him not to break his vow. The next day Arjuna wounded Bhishma, removing him from the battle.

In his philosophic outpouring of the first day, Krishna was Arjuna's teacher and counsellor. But in the events that followed the death of Abhimanyu, Arjuna's son, Krishna revealed the depth of his affection for Arjuna.

When Drona took over command from Bhishma, he sent a diversionary force against Arjuna, and then deployed the rest of his army in an intricate formation called 'the labyrinth'. Arjuna's sixteen-year-old son Abhimanyu was the only one left in the Pandava camp who knew how to penetrate the labyrinth. He managed to go in, but Jayadratha and others immediately closed the entrance again, trapping the boy alone inside. Veteran Kaurava warriors attacked Abhimanyu, killing his horses and his charioteer. He continued to fight bravely on the ground but was finally killed.

That night Arjuna returned to find the entire Pandava camp in lamentation. Weeping and raging he asked his brothers, 'How could my son be killed when you were all there?' He vowed that next day before the sun went down he would kill Jayadratha. Krishna protested, 'What do you mean, you are going to kill him tomorrow? Without even consulting me you have taken a terrible burden on your head. We will be the laughing-stock of the whole world.' Arjuna went on raving, so Krishna said no more. He brought Arjuna back to his camp, gave him his evening meal, and spread fragrant grass on his pallet. After talking a while with Arjuna, he left him and went to his own camp.

Jayadratha was not a great warrior and killing him was neither important nor difficult. But the next day, the whole of the Kaurava army would be devoted to his protection. If Arjuna failed, he would be bound in honour to commit suicide. Krishna could not bear that. 'I have my wives, my brothers, and my kinsmen,' he told his charioteer. 'None of them is as dear to me as is Arjuna. I could not live for a moment if something happened to him.' He would try his best, he said, to see that Arjuna fulfilled his vow. But if it appeared that Arjuna alone could not accomplish it he himself would take up weapons and fight. 'Keep ready my chariot and all weapons', he said, 'and bring it when you hear my conch. Tomorrow the world will see the test of my friendship with Arjuna.'

When Jayadratha heard of Arjuna's vow, he wanted to leave the war and return to his own kingdom. But the Kauravas persuaded him that he would be safe staying in the rear.

The next day, as Krishna had foreseen, the sole object of the Kauravas was to stop Arjuna from penetrating their lines to reach Jayadratha. The Pandavas, on their part, were trying to penetrate the enemy ranks where they could, in an attempt to clear Arjuna's passage. The first to attack Arjuna was Drona, who challenged him to a fight. With a rapid volley of arrows, Arjuna threw him into confusion and rode forward laughing, 'I am not going to fight you today'. Working with one mind, the horses, the charioteer and the warrior went forward, taking advantage of an open space in the enemy's momentary hesitation.

They fought on, till Krishna knew the horses needed rest. Unharnessing them, he pulled the arrowheads from their flesh, stroked them, and let them rub their backs on the ground. While Krishna was busy thus, Arjuna stood by and fought off the enemy. Again Arjuna and Krishna mounted, and the refreshed horses surged forward. A little before the sun set, Krishna sighted Jayadratha in the distance and pointed him out to Arjuna. Arjuna shot, and his first arrow penetrated Jayadratha's throat.

Arjuna's impulsiveness had cost Krishna a sleepless night and a day of extraordinary effort. The next time, Krishna gave Arjuna no chance to be swayed by a momentary impulse. Arjuna was fighting Karna, who was now the commander of the Kauravas. When one of Karna's wheels sank in the soft earth, he dismounted and tried to free it. Appealing to the Kshatriya dharma, he asked Arjuna to stop fighting until he could get back in his chariot. The appeal was just the kind to move the chivalrous Arjuna. But Krishna immediately shouted, 'Who are you to expect dharma? Where was your dharma when Draupadi was disrobed? Where was it when all of you in chariots killed the boy Abhimanyu?' If there had been the slightest impulse of pity in Arjuna's heart, the reminder of Karna's wrongs put an end to it. Without hesitation Arjuna drew his bow and killed Karna.

When Duryodhana, the last of the Kauravas, was killed, Krishna was given the task of going to Hastinapura to console Dhritarashtra and Gandhari. As he sat with the aged couple, messengers came and reported the conversation between the dying Duryodhana and Ashvatthama. They reported Ashvatthama had got himself crowned as commander of the Kauravas, and had vowed vengeance on the Pandavas. The Kaurava army had been completely defeated and dispersed. The whole of the Kaurava camp was deserted. Krishna realized that Ashvatthama must be planning some treachery against the Pandavas. Cutting short his conversation, he hurried back to the Pandavas' camp.

The whole camp was in revelry. With victory, all discipline had been forgotten. Only the Pandavas themselves were anxiously awaiting Krishna's return. Without telling them his suspicions he took the

Pandavas away, and had them spend the night in the deserted Kaurava camp. That night Ashvatthama and Kritavarma attacked the drunk and sleeping warriors. They killed Draupadi's brother and all her sleeping sons and set fire to the camp.

From the first day of the war to the last, Krishna had saved the Pandavas. In due time, the Pandavas were put on the throne of Hastinapura, and Krishna returned to Dvaraka. He had achieved all his life's aims: security for the Yadavas and for the Kshatriya class, the throne of Hastinapura for his friends, the Pandavas, and Vasudevaship for himself.

The next thirty-five years must have been the most tranquil period of Krishna's life. The end came suddenly and catastrophically.

The story of the end of Krishna and the Yadavas is confused. Part of it is probably historical, part of it is certainly overlaid with myth. It is said that some Yadava boys were playing when they saw many Brahmans approaching. To make fun of the Brahmans, they dressed one boy as a pregnant girl, brought 'her' solemnly to the Brahmans and had 'her' bow down to them. They asked them, 'Sirs, can you tell us what will be born, a boy or a girl?' The Brahmans saw through the trick and in anger at their disrespect said, 'This boy will give birth to an iron pestle which will destroy all the Yadavas except Krishna and Balarama.' The next day the boy delivered. The pestle was immediately pulverized and the powder was thrown into the sea. Then the king made a proclamation that henceforth no Yadava should be allowed to drink liquor. The city was frightened by all kinds of inauspicious omens. Krishna remembered how Gandhari had cursed him at the close of the war, 'In thirty-five years the Yadava clan will be destroyed.' Krishna and Balarama decided that all the Yadavas should go on a pilgrimage along the sea. Taking their wives, grown-up young people and immense quantities of food and drink, they went to Prabhasa. After eating they started on a great orgy of drinking. Suddenly a quarrel started. Satyaki sneered at Kritavarma, 'That wasn't very heroic, the way you killed poor Draupadi's sons in a night attack.' Kritavarma countered, 'I suppose it was heroic the way you killed Bhurishrava, cutting off his head after his arms had already been cut off.' From words they came to blows, and Kritavarma killed Satyaki. In revenge, Krishna's son Pradyumna killed Kritavarma. This triggered the old hostilities between rival clans and soon they were at one another's throats. Since they had no weapons, they pulled out handfuls of reeds growing by the shore, and the reeds turned to iron in their hands. These reeds had grown from the powdered pestle thrown back by the sea. All Krishna's sons were killed. In anger Krishna himself killed nearly all the Yadavas. Finally, two of the survivors, Daruka and Babhru, begged him to desist and seek out Balarama. They found Balarama sitting in an isolated spot under a tree. Krishna sent Daruka to Hastinapura to inform them that the Yadavas had been killed by the curse of the Brahmans and that Arjuna should come to Dvaraka. Krishna then turned to Babhru and asked him to take the women and children into Dvaraka to protect them from the Dasyus. Babhru started to do his bidding when he was killed by an iron pestle thrown by a hunter. Krishna asked Balarama to wait while he took the women and children into the city. Telling his father what had happened, he asked him to guard the survivors till Arjuna came. Then he went out to rejoin Balarama. He found Balarama dead. Sitting down under a tree in melancholy contemplation, he was killed by an arrow from the hunter Jara.

The story above is full of contradictions and absurdities. Neither the *Harivamsha* nor the Jain versions of the story are any less confusing. That the Yadavas were destroyed in a drunken quarrel is the core of all the versions. The curses of Gandhari and the Brahmans seem to be obvious later interpolations, as does the ban on drinking among the Yadavas. One of the most improbable aspects of the story is that Krishna, who had worked all his life for the welfare of the Yadavas, killed most of them himself.

Apparently, the Yadavas were outside Dvaraka on an outing when a quarrel broke out and they started killing each other. It seems that there were also hostile bands of people that chose this opportunity to attack. The grass that changed to iron could well have been stiff iron-tipped reeds used as lances and arrows.

After the massacre of the Yadavas, Balarama, as usual, was sitting bewildered and ineffective. Even on their last day, Krishna had to take the initiative in providing for the safety of the others. He brought the women and children into the city and returned to stand by Balarama, to whom he had been loyal all his life. He found Balarama dead. He was free to go back into the safety of the city but he chose to remain outside. This deliberate choice of death rather than safety fits into the role he had played throughout his life. He was Krishna Vasudeva, the resplendent one, the one who lacked nothing, the one who gave magnificently. He could not remain with the women and children, awaiting rescue by Arjuna. He could not live under the protection of anyone, even of the Pandavas. He welcomed death, as all other actions of his life, with conscious deliberation.

Though Krishna had been primarily the giver in their life-long friendship, after his death he was more than repaid by Arjuna. Arjuna came and heard from old Vasudeva the account of the Yadavas' death.[1]

The Pandavas settled the sons of Satyaki and Kritavarma in small kingdoms, and gave Indraprastha to Vajra, Krishna's grandson and only survivor. Just as Krishna said he could not live in a world without Arjuna, Arjuna and the others could not live without him. Leaving Parikshit, Arjuna's gransdon, on the throne of Hastinapura, they set out to die.

Krishna had died. The Pandavas had died. But Krishna was reborn. The Abhiras, the very people who destroyed Dvaraka, brought Krishna back to life by making him their god. As they gradually established kingdoms in western India, like all other newly come

---

1 Vasudeva died and Arjuna had the task of cremating him, Krishna and the other Yadavas. Then taking the women, children, and the treasure of the city, he started to return to Hastinapura. On the way, he was attacked by the Abhiras and robbed of some of the women and treasure.

rulers in India, they laid claims to Kshatriyahood. They took the name of their predecessors, the Yadavas, and made Krishna their god. The Abhiras were keepers of cows and they made their god a cowherd. Stories were elaborated about the child Krishna, stealing butter, playing pranks and making love to the milkmaids.

This transformation of Krishna is something of a paradox. The Krishna of the Mahabharata is wholly human, but his complexity and a kind of non-involvement in his most intense action make him hard to grasp. We cannot feel close to the Mahabharata Krishna. The cowherds made Krishna a god. Krishna's teaching is contained in the first six chapters of the *Bhagavadgita*. Even in these chapters, about half of it is later addition. In these verses, Krishna talks as a man to his friend who is caught in a terrible mental crisis and needs guidance. But it is guidance given to an equal and not a devotee. The teaching is free of the later *bhakti* (devotion) principle. It does not contain the wealth of philosophical terminology seen in the later chapters of the Gita. In many ways it is a simpler philosophy and also a sterner one. It fully endorses the ritual of sacrifices. We have seen how all Kshatriyas were keen on these performances for the sake of this-worldly and other-wordly considerations. The concept of a conscious self as separate from a body was well known and the concept of an all-pervading consciousness which is called *Atman* or just 'He', was also well known. This was coupled with a firm belief in rebirth according to one's merits and the possibility of not being reborn ever. Krishna told Arjuna, 'Do not be silly. All the people gathered here, including you and me, have been on the earth before and will be on the earth in future time. What dies is but the body, the self remains indestructible. Everything that *is* has death and everything that dies has birth, so you must not mourn because you are going to kill these warriors. For a person of the warrior class, to die or to kill in an open war is but the proper type of death. You cannot avoid bad actions by desisting from war. Other actions also have values. Nor can you desist from action as long as you live. The best way out is therefore to go on doing the actions which befall one because one is born into particular social circumstances, but the actions should be done without any desire for a selfish or other end. This is called *Yoga*. In this stage the mind is at one with the All-self, the body is doing actions without involvement, without an eye to their consequence. There is no joy at fulfilment, no fear or frustration because of failure. This ever-present awareness of the Atman, the All-soul, takes away values like goodness and badness from one's actions. You should always be aware of this, beyond all present miseries, joys and involvements.

This advice given to Arjuna did not bear fruit, because the two people Arjuna did not wish to kill by his hands were not killed by him. His arrow threw Bhishma, his grandfather, from the chariot, who lived for a few months more, and Drona was killed by Dhrishtadyumna and not by him. This shows that the advice was to a friend and not to a humble devotee as is represented in the later chapters of the *Bhagavadgita*.

Krishna remains an elusive personality for this very reason. He worked, he thought intensely, he advised others, but we do not find him downcast or mourning because his actions, thought or advice did not bear fruit. He danced in joy, he killed in anger his own kinsmen as we are told in *Mousalaparva*, but we do not find him mourning even after the terrible end of his clan. He made arrangements that the old, the very young and the women be taken care of, and then met with his death. This is what he would have called Yoga, this calm, this noninvolvement. This is why Krishna remains a figure for thought and search, but never touches one emotionally as do the other figures of this great epic. It might have been for this reason that when at last he was made into a god, he became a god with the warmest human qualities: the naughty child, the playmate of simple cowherds, and the eternal lover of all the young women of India.

11 The End of a Yuga

'Yuga' in Sanskrit means one-fourth of the cycle of the universe. There are four yugas: Satya, Treta, Dwapara and Kali. The earth with all the living beings is created at the beginning of Satya and is destroyed at the end of Kali, to be recreated at the start of a new Satya yuga. According to the Hindu beliefs, the Mahabharata war was fought at the very end of the Dwapara. The beginning of the Kali was the signal for the heroes to start their last journey. The Mahabharata thus marks the end of a yuga. 'Yuga' in modern usage stands generally for an era, epoch or age. I have used the word 'yuga' in the title in this modern sense. When I claim that an epoch ended with this war, I do not mean to say that everything in it came to an end or vanished. Certain social systems like the patriarchal household have continued almost up to the present day. The whole of the Krishna cult must have begun very soon after the Mahabharata war; while certain literary forms, like what the Mahabharata represents, are not found after it. The Mahabharata is the story of the quarrel between cousins for the possession of property and status. This quarrel has been fought on various scales in all Indian families from then to the present. Though this theme is universal to a patriarchal society, this particular epic is about a Kshatriya family. Other than the Kshatriyas, there are many Brahman families and persons in the story. The other two classes, namely the Vaishyas and the Shudras, are very meagrely and vaguely represented. The relationship of the two prominent classes to each other shows rivalry as well as mutual dependence. The Kshatriyas needed the services of the Brahmans to propitiate the gods, to officiate at the life-cycle rituals and to perform the great sacrifices proclaiming their victories, glory and munificence. All the Brahmans, barring a very few, needed this sort of patronage and protection from the Kshatriyas. The few Brahmans who were known as great teachers and maintained forest-schools or were great philosophers, though independent to a certain extent, still enjoyed the privileges of Kshatriya patronage. The rivalry between these two is best illustrated by the story of Drona and of Parashurama. Not much is known about the Vaishyas and the Shudras. To judge from the *Bhagavadgita*, the Vaishyas were supposed to have been engaged in farming, herding cattle, and trade; while the Shudras were the servants of all the three classes. In later times, the positions of all the classes changed and shifted. At the rise of Buddhism and Jainism the social position of the Brahmans became lower. The Vaishyas, as the rich supporters of these two new monastic religions, gained in importance. Their status became so exalted that they, instead of the Kshatriyas, became heroes and heroines of Buddhist and, more specially, of Jain stories. Due to this rise in importance, the Vaishyas gave up the hard work of farming and cow-herding and became exclusively traders, moneylenders and landowners. The Shudras took over farming, minor artisanship and all the other occupations requiring hard labour. Up to the time of the Mahabharata war all the rulers were Kshatriyas or, in rare cases, the illegitimate sons of Kshatriyas (like Karna). After the Mahabharata war, however, many of the famous rulers belonged to other classes.[1] Apart from these, there was an ambiguous group of people who did not belong to any class. They were the mercenary or professional soldiers. Their service could be bought or they could be lent to others by their masters (as were the soldiers called Narayaniya, given to Duryodhana by Krishna). A branch of these soldiers was known as Samsaptakas, who had sworn not to show their backs to the enemy and who engaged Arjuna for almost half the duration of the war. Thus they could be bought and sold like the Shudra slaves and yet their profession was fighting, like that of the Kshatriyas. The Kshatriyas were primarily a ruling class who could fight or not fight according to their wishes. Such a choice was not given to the mercenaries. They make their first appearance here, and are found throughout later Indian history.

---

1 Pasenadi of Kosala (500 to 600 B.C.) was a non-Kshatriya, but it is not known to which class he belonged. Chandragupta Maurya (300 B.C.) was a Shudra. Harsha (600 A.D.) was a Vaishya. Besides these famous kings there were many other minor ones, including Brahmans like Shunga and Kanva.

The four *varnas* are mentioned by name in the Mahabharata. Castes, that is to say *jatis*, do not find a mention as castes, but there is no doubt at all about the existence of such endogamous groups. One such group was suta. The sutas had a definite place, not within the hierarchy of castes but within the framework of varna, as is made clear by Shalya, who said, 'Shudras are the servants of Brahmans, Kshatriyas and Vaishyas. Sutas are the servants of Brahmans and Kshatriyas but not of Vaishyas.' Thus their position was inferior to the two upper varnas and higher than the two lower ones. They married among themselves. They had life-cycle rituals apparently different from the others and that was exactly the point stressed by Karna in his talk with Kunti when he said, 'What is the use in acknowledging me now? I have grown up among the sutas and none of the Kshatriya rites (*samskara*) have been performed for me.' Kunti, having realized the force of this argument and anxious to do well by Karna at least regarding his last rites, insisted that he be cremated according to Kshatriya traditions. Many women from lower castes married Kshatriya kings and became queens. Their children were Kshatriyas by patrilineal law, but neither they nor their kin changed caste. One of the most important people mentioned in the Mahabharata are the Nagas, who were rulers and were called kings. Their daughters married into Kshatriya houses, but their place in the hierarchy of caste is never made clear. They definitely were not Kshatriyas. Another type of people often mentioned had the same names as some birds and beasts and were sometimes described as such.[1] They were jungle people (apparently) with clan-names of birds and beasts. These forest people still remain more or less on the same terms with the peasant society around them as they used to in the Mahabharata times. The caste society in its fullness is not represented in the Mahabharata, as the story primarily concerns the Kshatriyas. It may not have been as complicated as in post-Christian times, but it certainly was in existence.

As against the blurred background of the caste society the picture of a patriarchal Kshatriya family is clear and fully drawn to the last detail. Each ruling family was located in a capital city for generations, so that it came to be known as the house belonging to that capital. There was the House of Hastinapura and also others like that of Virata. The family lived in an enclosed courtyard, where, apparently, important members like the head of the family and his sons had separate houses. There were smaller quarters for other members. Vidura, the low-born half-brother of the ruling king, seems to have had a house outside the king's courtyard (*rajangana*), but within calling distance so that he could be summoned at any time of the day or night by the blind king. The family consisted sometimes even of four or five generations. The descriptions show that the various sub-families in the Hastinapura house did not cook or eat their food in the same place. This was possibly also the case with the Yadavas and other large Kshatriya households. Where the household was small, the picture is more like that of the present joint family.

---

1 Khandava Daha.

The kinship terms in the Mahabharata were only the primary terms: father, mother, terms for cousins, (male or female), uncles and aunts. This lack of distinction between one's own son and one's brother's son seems more poignant to modern eyes when Dhritarashtra makes the distinction by saying, 'the Pandavas are also my sons but Duryodhana is the one born of my body. How can you ask me to sacrifice my own body for those others?' The conventions which had to be followed seem cruel to us today as in the case when Dharma, before leaving for Varanavata as a young prince, had to come, and touch the feet of Dhritarashtra and Gandhari, address them as Father and Mother, and ask for their blessing, knowing full well that he was being sent to his death by them. The tables were turned at the end. Dharma killed all the hundred sons of Dhritarashtra in battle and became the king of Hastinapura. At that time Dhritarashtra and Gandhari naturally wanted to leave the palace and go to live in the forest. Dharma touched their feet, called them Father and Mother and asked them to bless his house by living there. The same convention then forced them to comply and continue to live in the palace for at least a few years. The men in a family were all born in it (other than the adopted ones), and the women were brought in from other families as brides. The women born in a family were given to others in marriage. The women's quarters were apart from the men's, and women did not normally go into men's assemblies. Even among women, the brides had a separate establishment from the daughters of the house. The two worlds that made up a man's universe were his own family and the families he was connected with through marriages. One's father's family was the most important, but if it was split by internal strife, one would always depend on the in-law families for support. The elders of one's family tended to avoid quarrels. They even countenanced injustice, but tried to suppress open disagreement and contention. Mostly they were of the opinion that one should not insist on getting one's own share of the father's property. They felt that if it were acquired without much resentment and bitterness, well and good; but this right should not be insisted upon at the price of family solidarity. The in-laws, on the other hand, were always ready to fight on behalf of the son- or brother-in-law. All the Pandava allies were their in-laws; the Yadavas were their mother's family, the Drupadas, the wife's family, and the Viratas, the daughter-in-law's family. And the one who tried so hard to help the blind Dhritarashtra and the Kauravas was Shakuni, Gandhari's brother.

During the Mahabharata times, the ideal of a woman's loyalty to her husband differed slightly from that of later times. It was customary then to acquire a son begotten by another man on one's own wife, if one happened not to have an heir. This was called niyoga and was considered a method superior to adoption, which later on replaced niyoga completely. In the Mahabharata times a woman was the 'field' and she had to produce children from any man when her husband demanded. This compulsion to produce sons disappeared later on with the popularity of adoption, but along with it also disappeared the tolerant attitude towards any lapse a woman might commit. Women who were rescued from the hands of the enemy and perhaps were used by them, were never abandoned. They were brought back into the family and given their former status. This attitude was not due to compassion. A woman was a man's possession. Inability to protect her from the enemy and losing her was a matter of humiliation to him, and rescuing and regaining her a matter of pride. This attitude was in complete contrast to the later one and to that of the modern Hindus who refused to accept their rescued wives when they were brought back from Pakistan.

The patriarchal family was the mainstay of the social order. The social values of those days, too, were such as to support this social order. The ideal virtues for men were devotion to one's father and good fellowship for one's brothers. These were the virtues that would protect and promote the welfare of the patriarchal family. The women who became part of such a family were brought from outside. They were expected to be devoted neither to their fathers nor to their brothers. They were to cultivate the virtues of devotion to their husband and take pride in his family. A woman's loyalty to her father's family lasted until her marriage. After that her duties were to safeguard the name of her husbands's family, to care for all his children as their mother, to go where he would and to serve the parents-in-law.

The picture of the social order is definitely male-dominated and class (Aryan-Kshatriya) oriented. It was not as if they were not aware of moral or social values applicable to humanity as a whole. The *Bhagavadgita* clearly shows that a wider concern existed. But generally the values were narrower; which prevented them from realizing the cruelty involved in burning a whole forest with all the living creatures in it. Not that such atrocities are any rarer today, but there is always at least a section of the world which find them wrong and protests against them. None found anything to criticize in Krishna's and Arjuna's actions when they burnt the Khandava forest.

That values are always relative to time and place is the stand taken by Indian philosophy. And even their acceptance might be more theoretical than practical. For example, genocide is now recognized as an international crime and yet it is still committed and connived at. The great saint Tukaram admonished that 'Slaves be treated as kindly as one's own children.' A modern man instead of admiring the compassion behind this statement would indignantly point out how Tukaram condoned a society which allowed a man to own slaves!

The events in the Mahabharata, therefore, must be judged in the context of their time and place. We have already seen how the conception of the chastity of women was rather elastic in the Mahabharata times and became more rigid later on. Another incident in the Mahabharata which we cannot understand from our present position regarding right and wrong, is the alliance of Shalya, the king of Madra, with Duryodhana. This meant going against the Pandavas of whom the youngest two were his sister's sons. The first difficulty, of course, concerns the kinship terms. The word 'sister' might have meant a sister or a distant cousin. If the latter was the case, he was related to both the sides in an equal degree. It cannot have been that he resented the fate which had befallen his young sister, who had burnt herself on Pandu's funeral pyre. There is no evidence to support the suspicion of such a resentment and neither can we expect it, for what Madri had done was only the conventional thing. This whole war was so peculiar that as far as allegiance went, it depended rather on the closeness of the blood- or marriage-relationships than being on the side which was right. But then most alliances in all wars depend rather on issues other than on which side was in the right. The two values which Bhishma exalted above personal goals were, on the one hand, the broader one of family welfare and, on the other, the extremely narrow one of a self-imposed ideal, which it would have been better to have discarded, if the broader value were to be given more importance. But he was prepared to put an individual value above a social one and stick to his vow of celibacy in spite of the fact that by doing so he was to harm the future generation of his family. Each character in the Mahabharata was aware of the framework of moral values and when faced with a choice, chose according to his or her lights.

The political system of those times was only an extension of the social system. There were small, jungle-surrounded kingdoms ruled by hereditary kings. It was considered wrong to annex other kingdoms to your own by conquering their kings. Jarasandha, the king of Magadha, who called himself Samrat had apparently defeated the neighbouring kings, put them in prison and appropriated some of the kingdoms. Dharma had to first conquer Jarasandha before he could acquire the title Samrat or perform the Rajasuya sacrifice. We are told that he did all these things, but without depriving any king of his hereditary kingdom. Jarasandha and Shishupala were killed at this time, but the kingdoms were given to their sons. A king who performed the Rajasuya had to defeat a few kings in battle, some he won through friendship, and others agreed to his being called samrat because they were his kin. He had to invite and honour all the kings, give them gifts, feed thousands of Brahmans and perform the sacrifice with due pomp and ceremony. It is comparable to the 'Potlatch' ceremony performed by the Kwakiufla Indians. Poets have sung of the impecunious circumstances to which great kings were reduced after performing this sacrifice. 'Samrat' meant the best among kings. In one family the Rajasuya could be performed only once in a generation and none else could perform it while that man lived. Though Duryodhana succeeded in usurping Dharma's kingdom and driving him away, he could not perform the Rajasuya, even though he wanted to. After the Mahabharata age, great empires were founded in northern India. During Buddha's time King Pasenadi of Kosala was a great emperor. Magadha itself was the seat first of the Maurya and then of the Gupta empires. These later samrats were sovereigns over other kings. The meaning of the word samrat as 'the first among peers' was lost. Such small kingdoms existing on the basis of mutual respect were found in ancient Greece and in Europe even up to the medieval times. The small German kingdoms which existed right up to the time of Bismarck could not have been any larger than the states described in the Mahabharata. Even today, after large empires have had their day, our problem is the same as that of the Bharatiya kings, namely co-existence.

The gods of the Mahabharata are vedic, classical or puranic. Even temples are not mentioned.[1] Hymns in the praise of Shiva, the thousand sacred names of Vishnu and the many names of the Sun-god which occur seem to be later interpolations. Of these three deities the Sun-god was the most ancient. Shiva came later and the thousand-named Vishnu seems to be the last. The ritual in the Mahabharata was based on sacrifice. The king's priest had every day to make offerings to the sacred fire, who, as a messenger, carried them to the other gods. In all big sacrifices, animals were slaughtered and offered to the fire. Still, the institution of sacrifice was not developed to the extent it was in the later centuries. Indra, Surya and Rudra were the chief deities. People believed in heaven, or a place presided over by Indra. The idea of hell was not so distinct, though obviously in existence. Offering was

---

1 The word *'Devayatana'*, (god's house) is mentioned four times: (*Adi*- 64, 40; *Bhishma* -108, 11; *Anushasana*- 10, 18; *Ashvamedhika* - 69, 15) All these seem to be later additions.

made once every month to the dead ancestors. The doctrines of *karma* (result of one's actions) and rebirth were firmly established. Apart from this, there are many discussions in the Mahabharata on dharma and non-dharma, on Atman and the world. In spite of these arguments, a clear definition or description, or the inner meaning of the word dharma does not emerge. This attitude of intellectual inquiry was later lost. *Bhaktimarga* (the way of devotion) blunted all search. Apart from the later faiths like Vaishnavism, Shaivism, Buddhism, etc., the main stream of religious thought remained nameless, elastic, fluid and individual. The name Hinduism, by which it is now known, was given to it by foreigners. Even today, no thinking Hindu will be able to give a clear-cut definition of his religion. All he would say is 'This is *my* interpretation'.

Nowhere else does one find so many discussions about what is dharma and what is not, as in the Mahabharata. In works like the Bible and the Quran there is a categorical statement of what religion consists in. In the Mahabharata there are questions, answers and doubts regarding the nature of religion and human destiny. That is the reason this story comes so close to us. In the last thirty years, Western literatures reflect a mood of questioning. They question the value and meaning of human existence and express despair at its futility. One feels that this revulsion is the effect of the death agonies and loss of empires and their glories. The more real and poignant is the realization of the emptiness of human success felt by Dharma and Arjuna. At the moment of victory, Dharma said, 'This victory seems to me as defeat.' And Arjuna was confident of destroying the enemy, but he too said, 'I do not wish to kill them, even if they kill me. I would not want to kill them even for the kingdom of heaven, let alone for this small piece of earth.'

Krishna gave a two-pronged answer to the dilemma of Arjuna. His first answer, saying that the Kauravas were unjust and deserved to die, was not heeded. Therefore he went on to elucidate the valildity of human action in relation to the ultimate reality. He said that though reality was the ultimate goal, it could never be reached without taking a definite stand about human life. The human society and its values had a validity provided that values did not become the means of personal aggrandisement. The non-attachment described by Krishna regarding the world was not of the same kind as that of the 'Stranger' or the 'Outsider' one meets in modern literature. Krishna says that since it is not possible to remain a mere 'witness' and not to be involved in any action, it is better to act with complete self-knowledge and with the results of the action in view.

At the time of the Mahabharata, the bhakti cult had not begun. Arjuna was not a devotee of Krishna in the later sense of the word, only his very dear friend. This is seen by the fact that no amount of persuasion on Krishna's part could prevail upon Arjuna to kill the two old men he had refused to kill. With great reluctance he agreed only to disable Bhishma so that he fell from the chariot; and neither did he kill Drona, who was killed by someone else. He did not kill them himself but saw them die. He witnessed the deaths of many others and lived to see even his dearest friend Krishna die. For his own death he chose to go as far and as high in the Himalayas as his feet would carry him and to die where he would fall. Others too, Kunti, Draupadi, Dhritarashtra, Gandhari, and the other Pandavas chose to die in this way. They all drank their fill of the joys and sorrows, honour and dishonour in life. They struggled, they sacrificed much, but not because they hoped to gain anything extraordinary. The matter and the style of the Mahabharata is suited to this harsh, bare, stark and demanding philosophy of life.

The values, gods and literature of the later epoch are totally different. On the one hand, sympathies were enlarged to include the whole of mankind, on the other hand thought lost its logical tightness. Pity for others is an expression of the pity one feels for one's self. Heidegger has put it very neatly. *Dasein* is destructible by its very nature and in its birth carries the seed of its death.[1] 'Being' is constantly afraid of 'Not-Being.' He tries to make believe that this fear of his is on account of others and not on his own account and is, as a result, filled with anxiety for the whole world. The sight of sickness, old age and death turned the Buddha away from this world. He advised non-attachment for he believed that the more the involvement the more the

---

1 Dnyaneshwar, a 13th century Marathi poet, has expressed this same thought as follows: 'When (in the world) the sun rises only to set and where the moment of conception determines the moment of death.' *Dnyaneshwari*, 9, 497-98.

anxiety and fear. The teachings of the Mahabharata are diametrically opposed to this. True, all these philosophies are based on the premise that 'what is born must die',[1] but the Buddha and Krishna go on to say, 'and all that dies must be born again'. Heidegger does not go this far. The stand emerging out of the same premise says: whatever is, is this world, as you see it, there is no future and no past; therefore, think only of the here and the now, there is no sense in talking about values. This is the stand taken by the existentialist writers of today. The philosophy and ethos offered by the Mahabharata are firm and hard; that of the Buddha are not merely escapist but also full of internal contradictions. Buddhism asked people to abjure the world and become monks, but ignored the fact that a wealthy and charitable merchant-class engaged in the business of life was needed to support these non-attached monks. The stand of the existentialists is one of defeat and despair. The last two are full of pity for the human condition. Even the harshness of existentialist literature is due to the firm belief that human life is meaningless. What was absent from the Mahabharata, but is found from the time of the Buddha up to now is hero-worship and unquestioning obedience to the order founded by the hero. 'I surrender myself to the Buddha, I surrender myself to the Sangha, I surrender my self to dharma', was the Buddhist chant, and is in other forms much in evidence today.

This hero-worship is at the root of the bhakti cult.

---

1 *'jatasya hi dhruvo mrityuh' Bhagavadgita* II.27.

Man hoped that the hero-figure or 'god' might be able to rescue him from the pointlessness of life. This hope in turn gave rise to two kinds of literature. The kind not found in India was the inflammatory, fanatical propaganda literature, mostly based on the worship of a 'Leader' or a 'Prophet'. The other kind, found all over the world, was sentimental and sweet, where 'god' always fulfilled one's heart's desire and whose help was available in times of difficulty. The idea of kind-hearted gods, devotion, monothesim, escape from reality, all these are not found in the Mahabharata; they all came later. In this sense the Mahabharata marks the end of an era. India retained her polytheism, did not give in to fanaticism, but made up for the lack of these two by abounding in sentimental, dreamy literature. The pervading despair and frustration, hardness and realism of the Mahabharata never again appeared in Indian literature. Some examples would make this contrast clear.

Bharata, the first dramatic theorist, laid down the rule that a play must not end tragically. Later dramatists stuck so faithfully to this norm that even what was originally a tragedy, the Ramayana, was made into a comedy. The hero, the heroine and their children were brought together in a happy family re-union at the end. *Vikramorvashiya* and *Shakuntalam*, written by the great Kalidasa, have the same banal ending. The picture of the present day American society shows a similar contrast between the real and the ideal. Even though the breaking up of families is a daily occurrence, much publicised in all the newspapers, the ideal of a close family is still clung to and all the political figures are expected to conform to it. Each candidate for any public office is displayed with his wife and children. In most Sanskrit classical dramas, the hero, a middle-aged, much-married king, runs after the prettiest handmaiden of one of his queens. Then he is separated from her and is at last re-united with her much later as the mother of his son. All is make-believe: love, the pangs of separation and the last family re-union. The pity of it all is that these comedies have been written by truly gifted poets whose poetry touches our hearts if only we can forget the context. A comparison between the Shakuntala story in the Mahabharata and in the later drama *Shakuntalam* by Kalidasa illustrates this point well. In the Mahabharata, the king and Shakuntala both were shrewd and cunning, out to get what they could. She gave birth to a son and when he grew up, went with him to his father's court. It is clearly stated in the Mahabharata at this stage that the king recognised her and yet denied ever having seen her before, for fear of scandal. Then heavenly voices proclaimed the boy as his son. The king was without an heir and so he gladly accepted the boy and the mother. This story shows the true character of those involved. It is a straightforward story, which fitted into the moral pattern of the day. Kalidasa on the other hand turned this somewhat sordid and mercenary story into a beautiful dream-like play. The poetry of his *Shakuntalam* is unforgettable, but it has lost the razor-sharp characterization of the original. There is nothing in it comparable to the court scene in the Mahabharata, featuring the speeches of mutual recrimination by the two calculating central characters. Kalidasa has depicted his heroine as an innocent, pastoral maiden. Even the king is white-washed through a far-fetched curse which makes him lose his memory and forget her temporarily. The last reunion is so stereotyped that it would have become unreadable had it not been for the beautiful poetry. Every emotion in this tradition is described in an exaggerated manner. The longing of Draupadi for Arjuna is expressed in the Mahabharata in a couple of stanzas. One burning, acid and bitter verse relates Kunti's terrible jealousy for her co-wife and pity for herself. And a mere sentence suffices to reveal Karna's fruitless striving. The classical literature is sweet in sound and sentiment, but illusory, while the Mahabharata is concise, hard, unpolished but intellectually and emotionally profoundly disturbing.

In a pre-Mahabharata book called *Aitareya Brahmana* appears the story of Rohita, the son of King Harishchandra. Its treatment here is so different from the later (post-Mahabharata) puranic version that both are worth citing for comparison. Harishchandra was heirless. He prayed to the god Varuna for a son, and promised that should there be a son, he would be given to the god. Varuna gave him the son. The boy was named Rohita. From the moment the child was born, Varuna claimed him again and again, but the king sent him away each time, first with one excuse and then with another. When the boy was grown up his father told him that he was to be sacrificed to Varuna. 'On no account', said the son, picked up his bow and arrow, left the house, and went into the forest. Another god,

Indra, advised him to keep to the forest for six years. Varuna, not getting his due, cursed the king with dropsy. Rohita, in the meanwhile, bought for the price of one hundred cows one of the three sons of a poor Brahman, took him to the king and asked that the Brahman boy be sacrificed in his stead. Varuna, when appealed to by the king, liked the idea of getting a Brahman boy and agreed to the exchange. The Brahman boy was tied to the sacrificial pole and the ceremony began. But none was ready to execute the boy. Thereupon the boy's father himself agreed to perform the deed on an additional payment of three hundred cows. Looking certain death in the face, the boy desperately prayed to all the gods, including Varuna. As he began to sing the hymn in Varuna's praise his bonds fell one by one. At last he was free and Varuna freed the king too from his promise and his disease. The Brahman boy, disgusted with his parents' behaviour, would not go back to them and was then adopted by the great sage Vishvamitra and himself later became a great seer.

This was the old story. In the Puranas, King Harishchandra had a dream in which he gave his kingdom to a Brahman. The next day the Brahman indeed came and demanded the kingdom. It is customary to give a Brahman something over and above the promised gift. The king sold himself and his wife as slaves to earn that extra money and gave that to the Brahman. The husband and wife were sold to different people. Rohita the son went with his mother. He later died of a snakebite; and while his mother wept over the dead body, the Brahman cast a spell and transformed her into what looked like a child-eating witch. She was condemned to death and the task of executing her fell to her husband Harishchandra, who was the slave of an executioner. When he raised his axe to kill his wife, suddenly all the gods and the Brahman appeared before him and stopped his hand. They praised the king for having kept his word to the bitter end. They restored his son to life and gave back the kingdom. He lived in enhanced glory ever after. The king in the *Aitareya* was a human being. He would not give his child even to a god, on any account. When afflicted by dropsy, owing to not having kept his word, he bought a substitute but would not surrender his own son. To save his son he broke his promise even though he had made it in person and that too knowingly to the god. The later Harishchandra who went to all kinds of lengths to fulfil a promise made in a dream, behaved contrary to human nature and ultimately when he regained all that he had given up and more, even the fulfilment of his promise proves to be illusory, and his vaunted honour appears quite hollow.

Not only this story but all the other stories, too, in later literature are of the same kind. A person is shown to possess one virtue to an excessive degree. Instead of this excess leading him to inevitable ruin, he is rewarded extravagantly in the end. The literature up to and including the Mahabharata is entirely different in tone. Take for example the story of the Mahabharata itself. The people in it do what they must, and pay for it when they have to. The wheel of life turns at a certain speed in one direction. The direction cannot change nor can the movement of the wheel be halted; men, women, kings, beggars, even gods cannot be liberated from the course of fate. They all have to see sorrow, hardship and ruin along with happiness, well-being and success. Bhishma could not escape this, nor could Dharma, nor Krishna himself. The Mahabharata is a history ('Thus it was') and while recounting what was, it also portrays the hopes, struggles, ambitions and despairs of the characters. But all emotion and strife are at a human level. No superhuman or divine agents come to rescue the people from their human plight. There was a tight framework of values and behaviour behind this literature. Whatever was done was done as a duty or as an unavoidable task. Nothing was done for the sake of happiness. If happiness there was, it was gained at the price of much sacrifice. In the battle the loser lost his life and the winner had but an empty victory. There is no scope in such a story for a contrived happy ending. There was no god who could fulfil all human desires. God and man alike were yoked to an inevitable fate which none could escape.

The limitations of life on earth are clearly stated; the Mahabharata did not create a dream-world where these could be transcended. Miracles did not occur, gods did not descend to change somebody's fate, and misfortune was not transmuted into good fortune. One did one's duty not because of any expected reward, but because one wanted to live with honour and to die with honour. This honour consisted in preserving the values inherited at birth. The word 'inherited' here is used deliberately. Apart from the values which were common to the whole of mankind, there were special values one had to guard because of one's position and birth. One was born as a Kshatriya or a Brahman in one caste. One was a mother, a daughter or a son. Each had to behave as was expected from a person in that position and each strove to attain the values implicit in that situation. The reward for keeping true to this hard discipline was not of the kind to be realised in human life or to be grasped by human hands.

In the later era everything changed. The ideals of truth, valour, fidelity, devotion were taken to extremes. The way in which characters were made to behave in order to reach these ideals and the ideals themselves, both ring false. The sorrows these characters suffered always proved transitory, while as a result of practising these virtues they got enduring happiness. Whether these people acted out of a respect for the values or for the reward good behaviour brings one does not know. Harishchandra, who sacrificed all, got it back and more. In the play *Uttararamacharita,* Shambuka, whom Rama had killed, comes back again more beautiful than before. The ordeal by which Sita vanished into the earth is also shown to be an illusion. Queen Changuna crushed her child to death, only to have it restored to her again. Every hardship was a test of one's goodness. If one passed the test, all that one had lost in the process was restored with added glory and honour. In this alchemy the hard outline of real life vanished entirely and in its place was created a dream world in which the hero and the heroine always lived happily ever after in spite of the grave calamities they had had to face. This epoch in literature continues to date. It belongs to men frightened of life, wanting out of literature what is impossible to obtain in reality. With the exception of some Buddhist literature, the philosophical discourse of Shankara, and a few stories, the rest of the literature is of the above type. It has its charm and beauty but none of it possesses the sharpness of the Mahabharata, nor anything else that provokes thought. The later bhakti literature is even worse because a story like that of Ajamila[1] undermines the very foundations of social values. People showed an excess of devotion not only to god, but to their earthly *gurus* as well. Before the Mahabharata, a teacher was always supposed to say to his pupil at the end, 'Whatever is good in me that alone should you imitate, nothing else'. But our saint poets like Dnyaneshwar, Tukaram or Ramdas advised a pupil to follow his teacher with blind devotion. After the Mahabharata period why did all literature become so soggy with sentiment? The ancients daily prayed to the Sun, 'Keep our intellect always on the go like a horse whipped by the master.' How could the descendants of these very people be content to hand over their thinking powers into the keeping of a guru? This is an unanswerable

---

1 Ajamila was an impious man who indulged in all the worldly pleasures, never did any good to anybody, and was utterly selfish. On his deathbed he happened to utter the name 'Narayana' which was the name of his son. It also happened to be the name of Vishnu, one of the principal deities. Because of this unintentional pious act, he was taken to heaven by the angels.

riddle in our social history. How divorced literature was from reality in the later age can be demonstrated by another instance. In the Mahabharata, friendship was possible only among equals. One can say that part of the story of the Mahabharata rose out of an incident where Drona, a poor Brahman, tried to claim the friendship of Drupada, a powerful king, on the strength of their having been the students of the same guru. Drupada rudely repudiated his claim of friendship but was willing to support Drona as a deserving Brahman. Drona never forgot this insult. Later, he wrested one-half of Drupada's kingdom with the aid of his pupil. This made the two of them equals and thus eligible for friendship. Duryodhana gave the kingdom of Anga to Karna and called him a friend. But Karna was a suta and so not of a status equal to Duryodhana. The remarks made by Shalya in *Karnaparva* show that to the very last, the relationship between Karna and Duryodhana was not one of friendship, but that of a retainer and a master. The third example of friendship is that of true friendship between Krishna and Arjuna. They were both social equals; they were Kshatriyas, younger brothers of kings, both had helped each other on many occasions, had shared confidences of feats performed in love and war and had got drunk together. Their friendship was what the Mahabharata considered the ideal kind of friendship. In those times only equals could become friends.

In later times, when godhead had been thrust upon Krishna, the story of his 'friendship' with one Sudama (not heard of in the Mahabharata) shows an entirely different idea from that found in the Mahabharata. Sudama was the son of a poor Brahman. He and Krishna were living in the house of the same guru. After finishing their education, each went his way. Sudama was a mediocre person. He remained a poor Brahman, and in addition was married to a shrew who made life miserable for him. She used to nag him to go and beg for some money from Krishna. In this later story, Krishna is shown to have been the king of Dvaraka. Finally, fed up with her nagging, Sudama went to Dvaraka. When Krishna heard his name, he went to him, embraced him and brought him over to the throne to sit near him. The queens attended to Sudama at the time of his bath and Krishna ate with great relish the handful of puffed rice that the Brahman had brought as a gift. When Sudama returned to his village, he found that Krishna had sent him a lot of money and gold. This story is known to every child all over India. It seems as if it was deliberately written as an antithesis to the story of Drona and Drupada. It might either have been written to drive home the moral that money and power should not bring contempt for the poor; or it might be an illustration of the fact that in the eyes of God (Krishna) the rich and poor are alike. This so-called friend entered Krishna's later life just once, and that too only for selfish reasons. According to the Mahabharata, this relationship cannot be termed 'friendship' and the story would illustrate only the principle of *noblesse oblige*. The concept of friendship apparently changed after the Mahabharata.

Up to the time of the Mahabharata, Sanskrit

literature comprised hymns, rituals, stories and long narratives like the Mahabharata; all original creations. The vast body of critical and explanatory literature belongs to the later period. All of it was based mainly on the earlier original thought. Not that there were no new creations, but they were far outweighed by the other kind. In a way this is true of all literature. The Mahabharata is the primary source of all the drama, poetry, fiction and criticism which came later.

The society shown in the Mahabharata was restricted in many ways. Their economy depended on agriculture and cattle. The Aryan newcomers had started to mix with the indigenous population, yet their cultural life remained confined to the original pastoral, and Indo-European way of life. Their favourite animal was the horse. The prestige of a Kshatriya depended on the number, quality and handsomeness of his horses. The names of many kings were indicative of their ownership of horses or of the coveted qualities in horses.[1] To be a charioteer and to fight from a chariot were considered great achievements. The chariots were drawn by horses and their wheels had spokes. The warriors of those times did not know horse-riding. That skill was introduced into India a thousand years later, at the beginning of the Christian era.

---

1 Haryashva (owner of a red horse); Ashvapati (owner of horses); Shvetavahana (one who is borne by a white horse; also one of Arjuna's names); Yuvanashva (a colt or the owner of some).

Tending of cattle and farming were the material foundations of life. One wonders if people used to eat beef. There is no definite evidence whether they did or did not. In times immediately before the Mahabharata, people did eat beef. In fact tender veal was supposed to be eaten on festive occasions, or was offered to an honoured Brahman guest. This sort of definite statement is not found in the Mahabharata. Professional hunters of game as well as hunting find a frequent mention. The Pandavas, during their exile, we are told, subsisted mainly on hunting. While in the forest, the Pandavas supported many Brahman dependants. One infers that they also partook of the game which was hunted and cooked. Bhima is said to have demanded meat every day. The many references to hunting lead one to believe that beef-eating had either disappeared or was extremely rare. All Kshatriyas owned large herds of cattle. They never sold milk. Were the cattle kept merely to supply the kingly household with milk and milk products and to provide the butter needed as an offering in the numerous sacrifices? Or was beef an occasional item of consumption? In the quarrel between Karna and Shalya (obviously a later interpolation), Karna condemns Shalya's country, Madra, because the people ate beef and drank liquor. (8.22.77) In the Mahabharata, all Kshatriyas drank freely. This passage condemning the north-western countries must have been interpolated after the land of Kuru-Panchal became the stronghold of later Brahmanical orthodoxy.

Various animal products are mentioned as appropriate offerings in the sacrificial fire to gods. Milk and milk solids and *ghrita* were some of these. Ghrita in later times came to mean butter-fat. But there is no evidence in Vedic literature for this interpretation. Ghrita simply means fat of a viscous consistency and could well have been cattle-fat (suet). The fat of other animals was also used, as the word *ajya* shows. This can be derived from the word *aja* meaning 'a goat', or from the verb *anj* meaning 'to anoint'. Goat-fat might have been used as a sacrificial offering and also as an ointment.[1]

What people eat, they offer to their gods, and inversely whatever is offered to the gods is consumed by the people. Horses and goats were certainly sacrificed then. And though cattle are not mentioned as having been an item of offering, new archaeological evidence does show that cattle too were used similarly. Does this mean that beef was eaten as a matter of course and perhaps for that reason finds no special mention, while game does?

The staple cereal food of those times was very probably *yava* (barley). This, too, was offered to the gods in a cake form, called *purodasha*. In their ritual, based on sacrifice, all types of cooked food including meats and cereals, was the traditional offering. Nowhere do we hear of the four things which are mentioned in the Gita as the means of worship. Those are leaves, flowers, fruit and water.[2] This verse must be a later

---

1 All Northern tribal people do use fat to smear on their bodies.

2 Throughout the classical period and right up to date these four items are used for *puja*, the worship of gods.

addition. What men and gods ate in the Mahabharata times was no longer eaten later on. The people and their gods, both changed.

Another matter about which no conclusion can be reached is that of script. Did these people know how to write? The Mahabharata does not refer to writing. There are many occasions where one would have expected such a reference if indeed writing was known. Messages were transmitted by word of mouth. Messengers were sent not with notes but with long verbal messages. Vidura sent a trusted digger to Varanavata with a message for Dharma. The message was very secret in this instance, so it could be argued that Vidura did not want to put it on paper. But in other cases not only were the messages not secret, they were to be broadcast openly to a lot of people. Even in those instances all the messages were verbal. When Arjuna (in *Virataparva*) told Uttar to find his weapons in the tree where the Pandavas had hidden them, he stood below the tree and described the weapons to Uttar so that his own bow and arrows could be distinguished from those of his brothers. One expects the weapons to have borne names, but they all had instead some distinguishing mark on them. Those with the golden dots were Arjuna's. Bhima's had golden elephants on them. Dharma's were adorned with the red ladybirds, Nakula's with golden suns and Sahadeva's with locusts. Similarly, the king's cattle were branded but whether with the king's name or not we do not know. This was the case with the Kshatriyas and is true of them right up to recent times. But even as regards other castes writing is not mentioned. Agricultural and pastoral pursuits can well be carried on without the knowledge of writing. The pre-Aryan Mohenjodaro culture had a script. The first written records of the Sanskritic people appear in the fifth century B.C. It is possible that at the time of the Buddha (seventh century B.C.), writing was known because the economy then was based on commercial and monetary transactions which require the use of writing. The Mahabharata makes no mention of ink, paper, or pens. Perhaps Maya, the asura (Assyrian?) knew writing; but this is merely a conjecture. The romantic story of Rukmini's marriage to Krishna belongs to this period, though it is narrated in the Mahabharata. All the later poets have written that she wrote Krishna a love-letter asking him to spirit her away from her brother's house. Considering that in those times writing was not known, it is impossible either that she could write such a letter or that he read it.

The houses were not built in brick or stone. The Indo-Europeans built in wood. The early Buddhist caves are said to imitate the original wooden, thatched structure of the Aryans. The literature about sacrifices describes many kinds of ritual constructions (*chiti*) for which bricks were used. Once people got to know brick-making, they could easily have used bricks for constructing houses, but they do not seem to have done that. Poor people probably built mud-huts as they do today.

These people who were so sophisticated in matters

of religion, philosophy and social values, were rather backward in material culture. They were like other Aryan people, for example the Semitic and Hamitic people of Babylon and Egypt. The Aryans possessed superior weapons and superior means of locomotion in their horses and chariots. On the strength of these, they were able to subdue Egypt and Babylon and rule over them for some time. People belonging to this same linguistic family went to Greece as well. The social structure and deities of ancient Greece bear a marked resemblance to those described in the Mahabharata. There are many significant differences too. The *Iliad*, a timeless epic like the Mahabharata, is also about a war and the society depicted is very similar to that in the Mahabharata. They too had small kingdoms, all the rulers of which were equal. Agamemnon was as harassed and fed-up as Duryodhana, nursing the tender pride of the various kings in his camp. The gods of Greece, however, are more interfering than our gods. The Greek gods quarrel among themselves and join rival groups. There the status of goddesses like Athene is independent and equal to that of the gods. In India, at least up till the Mahabharata times, goddesses or the wives of gods did not have a special or an independent place. Even though both societies were patriarchal, Greek women are depicted in colours that are more vivid, various and prominent. Whether in the pantheon or in human societies, Greek women doubtlessly played a more important role than did the Indian women. Even if our women are shown to be more exalted, they are rather stereotyped and monotonous compared to the Greeks, because we see only two of their faces: as wives and mothers. The Greeks have portrayed many unforgettable women in their various roles as mothers, lovers, wives, sisters or daughters. There is Clytemnestra who killed her own son because he had sacrificed her child; Althea who killed her own son because he had killed her brother; the loyal Electra[1] who roamed many countries with her fury-pursued brother; and Antigone who gave up her own happiness to become the eyes of her father in his old age. The Greek gods and goddesses too are more ill-tempered, impatient and cruel, compared to ours. The closeness and affection between brothers and sisters depicted in Greek literature, and its total absence from the Mahabharata makes one wonder if this difference was due to the original patrilineal society splitting into the

---

1 The Mahabharata does not show any similar instance of the affection between a brother and a sister. Generally, the only use a brother had for a sister was to marry her off to a powerful king and thus gain an important ally. Women did not seem to have kept any close ties with the father's house after their marriages. Even though there did not seem to be any affectionate ties between the brothers and sisters, a sister could apparently count upon her brother as a protector, as in the case of Draupadi and Gandhari. Still we do not find any fond conversations or confidences taking place between them and their brothers. In later times the same situation prevails in Sanskrit literature. But after the middle ages the festivals of Yamadvitiya and Rakshabandhana are based especially on the close and loving relationship between brothers and sisters. This same emotion is manifest today in much of the folk literature of India. It is also found in all literature today. Such sentiments were not to be found in the older Sanskrit tradition but were prevalent in the folk-tradition and they slowly seeped into the whole society and literature.

two branches found in India and Greece. It is also possible that Greek society was influenced by the matriarchy of its Egyptian neighbours. The Greeks too had various reigning houses, priests and slaves. When Greece became democratic, the voting rights were reserved for the upper classes. The slaves did not enjoy these rights. The same was true until quite recently of the United Sates of America. Many other Western powers too are democratic at home but imperialistic abroad. There are clear distinctions between what is ours and what is foreign, between our gods and strange gods and there is certainly the tendency to exercise our rights, but not give any to foreigners. All this existed then and exists today. But the writers of those times wrote frankly about these things. They had smaller societies in which inequality of this sort was taken for granted and none found in it anything to be ashamed of. Today many of the injustices and inequalities of those days persist, but we tend to hide them and ignore them. Many think that the old traditions should be discarded because they are inapplicable in modern times. This is not true. Old traditions and thoughts never become totally inapplicable to new situations; and modern practices are never so new that they do not retain a grain of the old. This is what anthropology tells us. All societies are worthy of study: old and new, close and distant, civilized and primitive. This study must, of course, be undertaken with a view to comparison and understanding. Neither should preconceived ideas lead a student into idol-worship nor into a frenzy of idol-breaking.

A friend wanted to know why, after starting with the Vedas, the Upanishads and the Mahabharata, our whole society turned such a somersault. How did we accept the dreamy escapism of bhakti or blind hero worship after having faced and thought undauntingly of the hard realities of life? How did the people who used to eat all meats, including beef, find satisfaction in ritually drinking the urine and eating the dung of the cow, and calling this quadruped their mother?

It is not possible for me to give an adequate answer to these questions. I have raised them to provide thought. Another friend, however, expressed the following comforting thought. He said that even though nothing else remained, we should be thankful that the language can still be understood, that we can still read and appreciate the Mahabharata. It might well have been like Mohenjodaro, where there are artefacts, representational records of all kinds, even something written; but all remain a mystery because we cannot read what is written. I am indeed fortunate that I can read today a story called *Jaya,* which was sung three thousand years ago, and discover myself in it.

Appendix

THE CLAN OF THE YADUS

The whole of the Yadu clan is not represented in the accompanying genealogy. Only the important names are included. This clan was very extensive and the Puranas are not agreed about it. *Harivamsha*, the main book about the Yadus, gives a very confused account. The present genealogy is taken from Pargiter's *General Survey of Ancient Indian Historical Tradition* (1922). The father-son relation is shown by a solid vertical line. Where the relationship is of a distant ancestor-descendant, the connection is shown by a dotted line. Chedi, Vidarbha, Bhoja, Vrishni, Andhaka, Shaineya were all sub-clans of one big patri-clan. The thing to note is that they married outside the Yadu clan as also inside it. Chedi and Vidarbha were independent kingdoms. The other Yadu clans, fleeing before Jarasandha's onslaught, went and settled at Dvaraka. Perhaps Mathura, their original home, continued to be governed by the descendants of Kamsa. From this genealogy one can understand the many names of Krishna derived from his different ancestors, e.g. Yadava, Madhava, Satvata, Varshneya, Shauri and Vasudeva.

The Genealogy of the Kurus

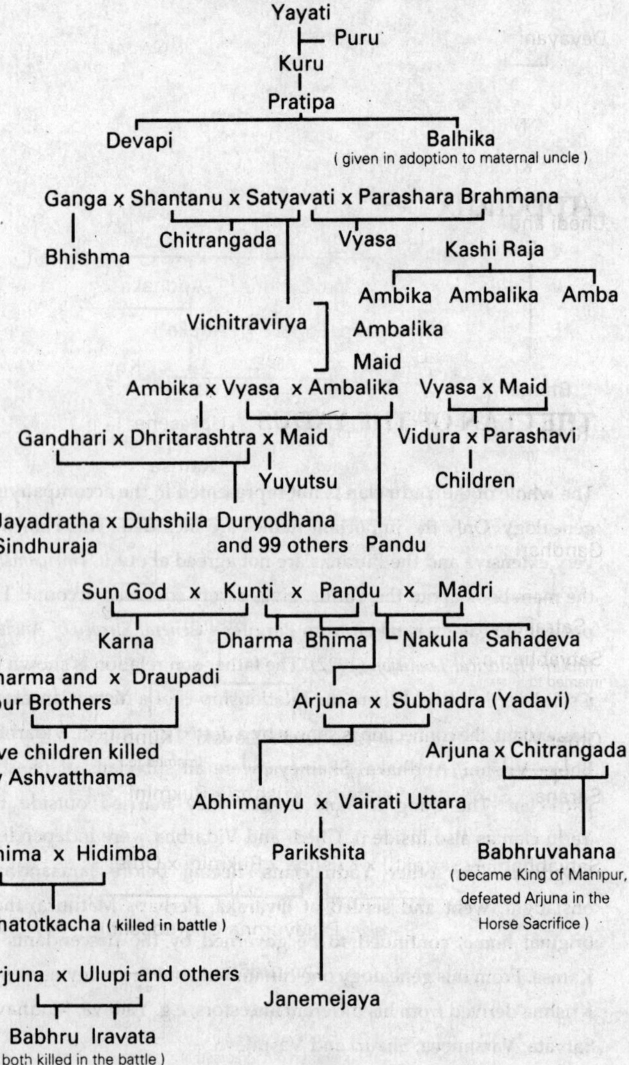

Clans related to the Kurus

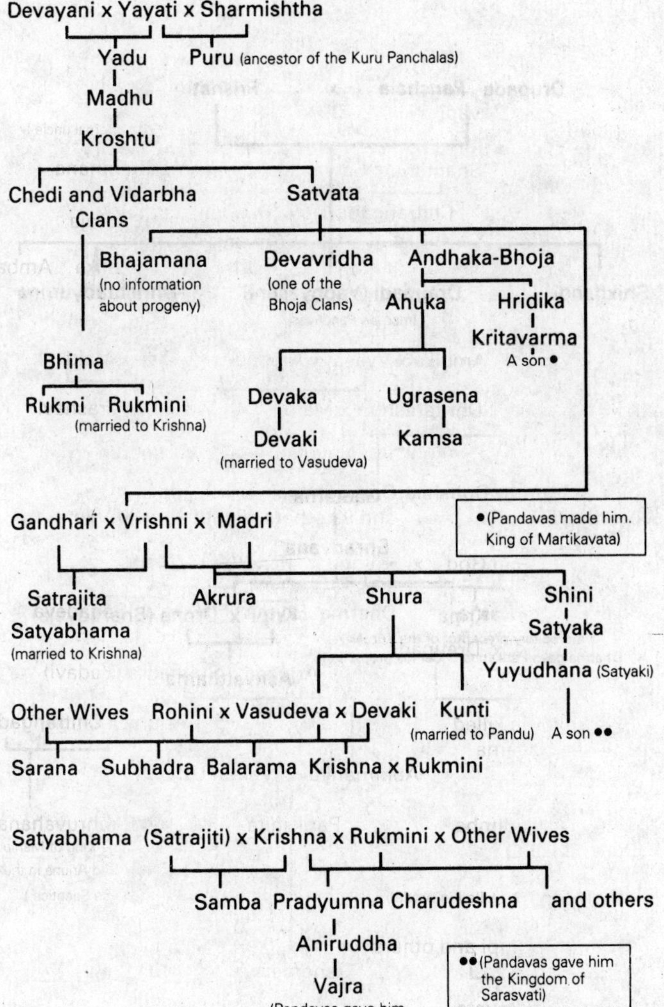

Clans related to the Kurus

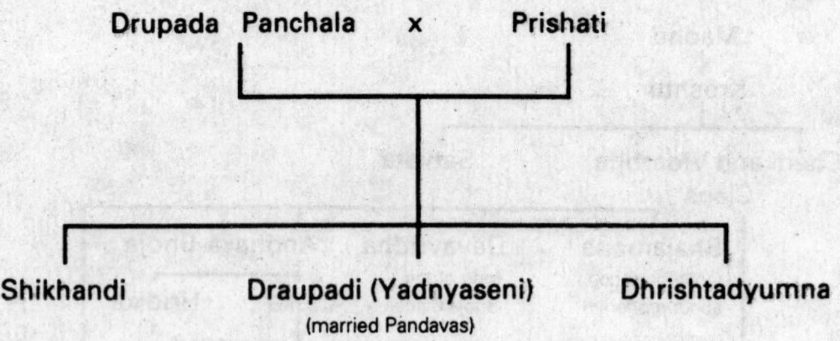

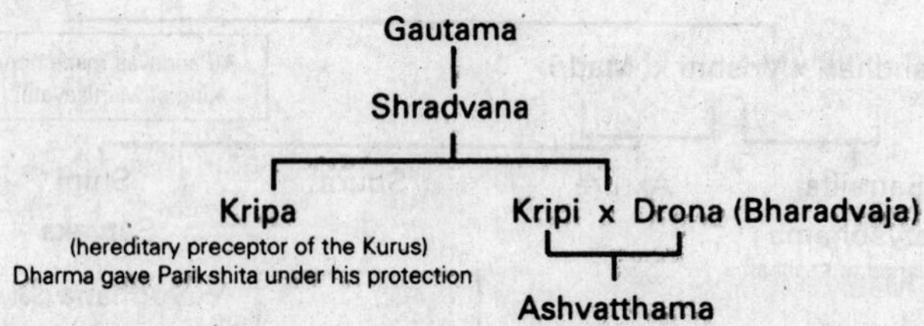

Clans connected with the Kurus

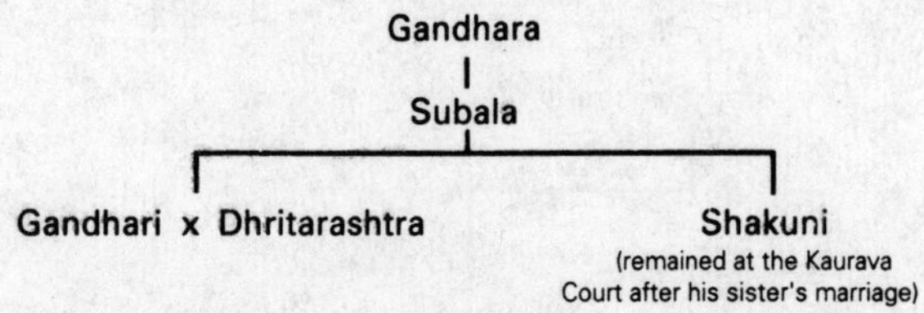

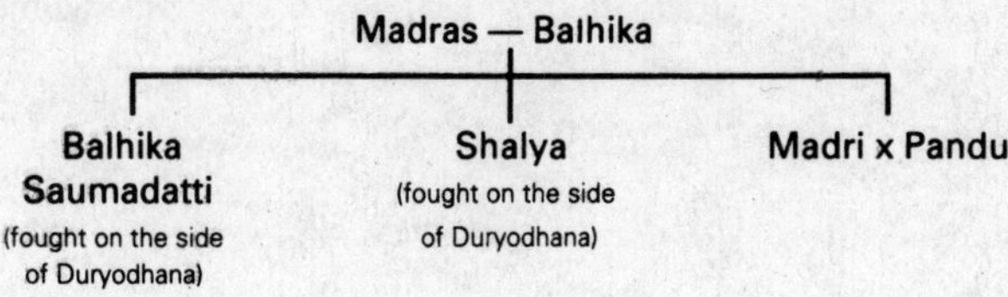

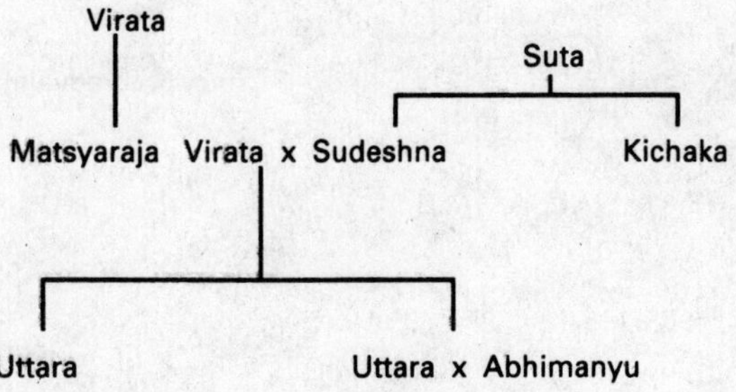

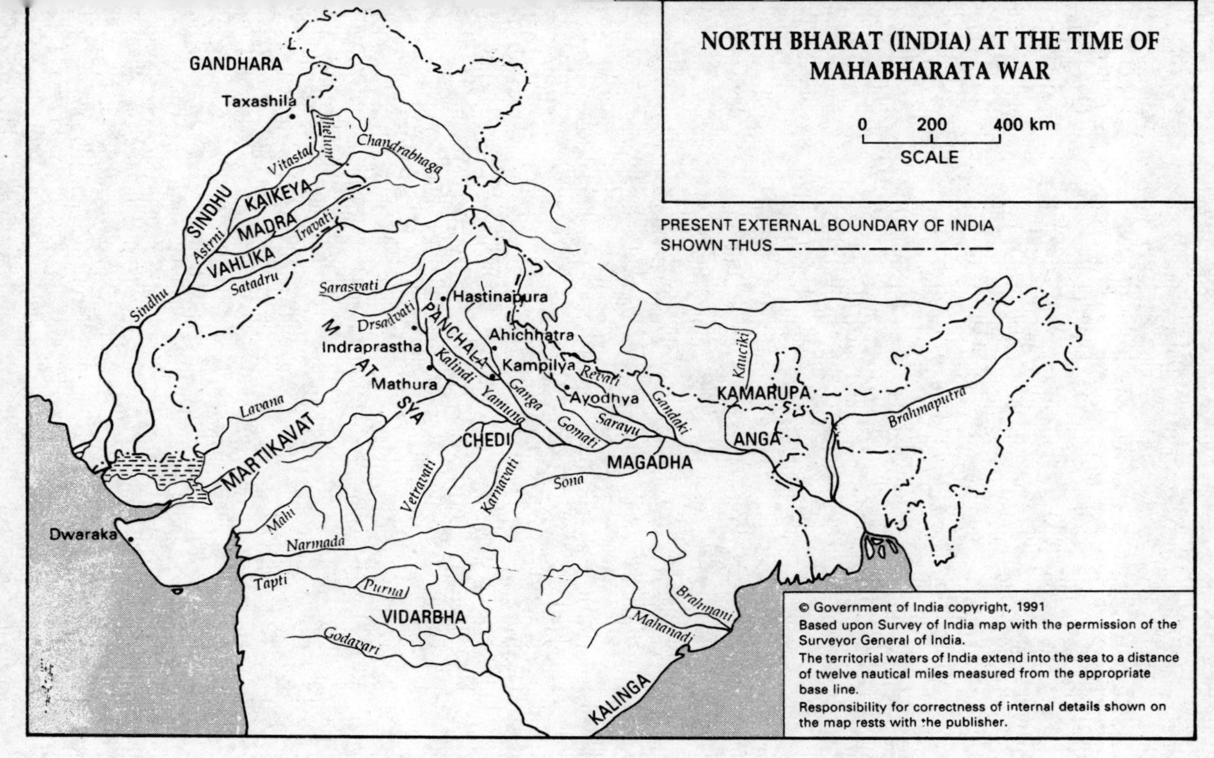
NORTH BHARAT (INDIA) AT THE TIME OF MAHABHARATA WAR
0
200
400 km
SCALE
PRESENT EXTERNAL BOUNDARY OF INDIA SHOWN THUS
GANDHARA
Taxashila
Jhelum
Chandrabhaga
Vitasta
SINDHU
KAIKEYA
MADRA
Iravati
Astrni
VAHLIKA
Satadru
Sindhu
Sarasvati
Drsadvati
Hastinapura
PANCHALA
Indraprastha
MATSYA
Ahichhatra
Kampilya
Revati
Kalindi
Mathura
Ayodhya
Yamuna
Ganga
Gomati
Sarayu
Gandaki
Kauciki
KAMARUPA
Brahmaputra
ANGA
MAGADHA
CHEDI
Lavana
MARTIKAVAT
Vetravati
Karnavati
Sona
Mahi
Narmada
Dwaraka
Tapti
Purna
VIDARBHA
Godavari
Brahmani
Mahanadi
KALINGA